WHAT PEOPLE ARE SAYING ABOUT

RISING FROM THE ASHES OF LOSS

I have known Mr Pierre Milot for approximately 30 years. In fact, he attended many of the activities we held at our Centre. Please check our website to have a better understanding of our focus: www.iiihs.org.

Pierre has always been excellent in his desire to learn, to study and to share. He is well qualified in a variety of areas including spiritual awareness, spiritual healing, hypnosis, near death experiences, spirit communication and counseling.

His desire has always been to be of service to humankind. His beloved wife Louise used to work with him in many areas. As a couple they were always willing to bring hope, courage, strength and truth to those in need.

The recent passing of his beloved wife enabled him to service what he had studied, what he knew and

His book is very moving, journey as he cared for, loved until she crossed the veil into the spiri

This book can provide a deep understanding of our journey on earth and how to face going from the darkness to the light.

Pierre's awareness of eternal life provided him where he needed to go, from sadness to joy.

This is due to Pierre knowing that there is no death...only eternal life.

Rising from the Ashes of Loss is a book which I feel can be of tremendous help to many people. Thank you for sharing your journey.

Marilyn Rossner PhD, EdD, International Institute of Integral Human Sciences

Rising from the Ashes of Loss

My Voyage through Grief

Rising from the Ashes of Loss

My Voyage through Grief

Pierre Milot

AYNI
BOOKS

Winchester, UK
Washington, USA

First published by Ayni Books, 2016
Ayni Books is an imprint of John Hunt Publishing Ltd., Laurel House, Station Approach,
Alresford, Hants, SO24 9JH, UK
office1@jhpbooks.net
www.johnhuntpublishing.com
www.ayni-books.com

For distributor details and how to order please visit the 'Ordering' section on our website.

Text copyright: Pierre Milot 2015

ISBN: 978 1 78535 151 8
Library of Congress Control Number: 2015939702

A CIP catalogue record for this book is available from the British Library.

Design: Stuart Davies

Printed in the USA by Edwards Brothers Malloy

We operate a distinctive and ethical publishing philosophy in all
areas of our business, from our global network of authors to
production and worldwide distribution.

CONTENTS

I dedicate this book to the two most important women in my life, past and present.
To Louise for being a trusting friend and loving companion for 38 years, and to Christine my new loved one, to whom I could never be grateful enough, as without her, this book would never have taken life.
Love
Always

Introduction

Present

It's ten o'clock in the morning. I just finished my morning coffee and I am sitting, lost in thought, on the cozy second-floor balcony of a rural cottage belonging to Christine, my new loved one. How strange it feels to say this without guilt, without feeling that I am not cheating on Louise, my wife of 38 years, who passed away from cancer just 18 months ago. It seems like such a short period of mourning before sailing on.

Christine's country house is the main setting in which my new book is coming to life. The cottage is situated by a gorgeous lake that inundates with clear pristine green water; a rarity these days. The sweet, delicious, and pungent scent of the nearby cedar trees, the joyful chirping of the birds nesting in the surrounding woods, and the picture-perfect view of the lake, with its waters clapping gently against the lakeside rocks, softly reawaken my senses and bring me back to life. Ah! To live again! So sweet to feel alive once more, something I never thought would happen after so much darkness and despair fell upon me when Louise died.

And, as if all these little delights were not enough, Christine's soft footsteps, climbing up the stairs to lovingly offer me a second cup of java, bring me further into the reality that there is life after loss. Beauty and love are possible once more to those who dare open up their hearts, and risk being hurt again.

How wonderful it feels to sit here and enjoy my new beginning. After 38 years of the near-perfect marriage, I thought that my time had come and passed, never suspecting that love would again spin its enchanting web in my neighborhood, offering me a second dance.

At a standstill between two sentences, as I decide what to write next, I notice a faint rustling in the branches of the giant pine tree ahead: two squirrels merrily run after each other. One jumps into a nearby tree; the other stands there, stamping its feet nervously, hesitating to take the leap. It seemingly decides not to, and friskily disappears the other way. How different would his life have been had he decided to make that jump? This scene, in appearance very mundane, is significant to me as it acts as a reminder that we constantly have to make choices in life, sometimes willingly and sometimes not, and that we will have to live with the consequences of those choices. If I stand here today, living, breathing and merging thankfully with life, it is because back then, when alone and in despair, I made decisions that gave birth to this possibility. I had reached the breaking point and considered ending it all, but I took the leap and chose life. I decided to stand up, dust myself off, and somehow muster up enough bravado to face another day, no matter how painful and miserable it could be.

After many deliberations, I elected to tell my story, to put it down on paper. This surely would be cathartic for me, I thought, and at the same time would hopefully inspire others to hang in there, to get the message that life gets better, no matter how despairing things may seem at any particular point in their tribulations.

Even though this book revolves around Louise and her courageous battle against cancer, it is really about me, the anxiety, the fear, the guilt, the pain, the joy, the hope and the anger I experienced while relentlessly accompanying her through three years of remissions and relapses, and finally to the end of her life. I want to tell the story from my perspective as sole caretaker, living in the life of my wife 24 hours a day, and how my whole life had become hers. I want to talk about how hopeful and thankful I felt in the times that she got better and how discouraged and angry and scared I became when the cancer had progressed again. I want to express the despair, the helplessness and the overwhelming sadness that engulfed me as she was slipping away through my fingers and, at the end, the hollowness I felt when she left me forever.

I want to describe how crushing and stuffy my house became as I was thrown into a debilitating loneliness and how, no matter where I went, whomever I was with, the knife, stabbing at my guts, would never go away. I want to ask my loved ones and friends for a little understanding when at times, during gatherings, I suddenly look distant, disconnected and not in the moment. I need to tell them that it is not out of lack of interest in them, but because I abruptly feel lost, disoriented and overtaken by a painful wave of sadness. I want to scream my anger and frustration at the medical profession, at God (whatever the heck that is), at me for not being able to do more for Louise, and shamefully confess the guilt I feel for miserably thinking, at desperate times, that Louise was not doing enough to help herself, when in fact she was fighting like a lion.

More importantly, I want to guide the readers through my journey of recovery after Louise's passing, how in an effort to overcome my grief, I relentlessly and stubbornly hung on to the practice of my favorite coping mechanisms. I want to talk about how and why I decided to meet new people so soon after I became a widower, and how I started to live again when I met Christine, the new person in my life.

I want to sensitize people to the idea that death and life are tied together, and to show that life is for the living, by talking about my own voyage. I want to demonstrate that I am not unique in my sufferings, that we all experience the pains and sorrows of loss, but that it is the way in which we process life events and losses that makes the difference between remaining bitter and angry and freeing ourselves to move on and grow. I do not want to nit-pick endlessly at a fate that has already been lived a million times before, but rather wish to bring encouragement and support to those who are caught in the same battle.

This book is not all about loss, pain and sadness. It is also about survival, fighting and winning. It demonstrates how to face loss, how to normalize grief, how to accept that death is part of the circle of life and, in the end, how we can experience joy and laughter again.

Anyone who has ever suffered or who is going through the destabilizing throes of grief knows what an energy drain it can be, and how the search for help and support must be brief, effective and to the point. In that regard, I feel privileged to offer my modest contribution and hope that my humble effort will be sufficient to bring my fellow sufferers the solace and encouragement they so badly need.

The stages of grief described in this book do not follow a specific order or pattern; I simply lead the readers through the stages as I experience them during my own grief journey. I use flashbacks to go from the pre-loss (past) and post-loss (present) phases of my voyage. The four appendices at the end of the book define the many aspects and types of grief and offer a detailed description of the different coping strategies that I used to survive and which helped me rise successfully out of the ashes of loss. I also brush briefly on the concept of abandonment and separation anxiety in the grieving process, from which, I'm afraid to admit, I'm still recovering.

I express the turbulent feelings that brewed inside of me during my trials and tribulations. This work would not be liberating otherwise. I also believe that it would not connect properly with other grievers who at times in their journey needed to scream out their pain and frustrations while in the midst of a difficult grieving moment, but did not, or if they did, felt ashamed for it. I want to normalize this aspect of grief and say to those people that it's OK to vent their feelings spontaneously and momentarily, as long as they don't let this behavior become obsessive. I want to apologize in advance if the reader finds some of my harsh words and criticisms offensive, but I still, to this date, have a bone to pick with the medical profession and some of the actors involved in my dramatic play.

This book may make you cry, laugh, trigger anger, shock you, take you places you may not want to go, lighten up your views on taboo subjects, even expand your understanding of life and death. It may do one or all of these things, but I suspect, at the very least, that it will not leave you indifferent.

My Story

Chapter 1

Post-Loss:
A time of denial, disorganization and confusion

November 29, 2010; the day after

Its 8 a.m. and I am just waking up from what I sense was a very short nap. Why does everything seem so weird, as if I were coming out of a dream? Why am I lying down in a hospital bed, although I do not feel injured or sick? My mind is in a whirl and I feel lost and confused. I look around in an effort to familiarize myself with my surroundings, when I suddenly realize that I'm in the middle of my living room...alone. My back feels a little damp from lying down on the rubber mattress that was left uncovered when they removed the cotton sheets...after they took her body away.

Louise died last night; the crude reality dawns on me now. My chest is suddenly pierced by a devastating stab and I begin to feel the debilitating pains of loss and emptiness that are to become my constant companions for months to come.

I remember, now that the dark fog clouding my brain is slowly dissipating: I slept in her deathbed last night in a desperate attempt to recapture her essence one more time. I can't tell if it helped or not, for I feel numb, disconnected and I don't remember much about the events that transpired after she passed. I try to lie down a little longer, hoping to connect with Louise yet again, but she is gone, never to come back. Death is so final. The house feels so big and hollow. I miss her presence so damn much it hurts and, with despair, I wonder discouragingly how I'm going to get through this.

Although a deep and relentless sense of sorrow is rapidly growing inside my being, as time passes I somehow manage to grasp at the last shred of strength and hope left in me. I get up, brush myself off, thinking, *Get up, buddy, this sulking in self-pity is not good for you. Go, get moving, do something, get away from the pain.* I know I was always a fighter and that I was never one to give in to the hardships of life; although I fear that this one is to test my resilience to the extreme, I must go on. *I won tough battles before*, I argue with myself in an effort to muster up enough courage and stamina to get out of my debilitating rut. I struggled to live through the trauma of abuse rained on me by my uncle when I was a kid, a situation that left me with an awful feeling of abandonment by my father who could not find the courage to protect me against my abuser. I also had to deal with the tragic accidental death of my teenage son which just about destroyed me. I will somehow wrestle successfully through this too.

Although I had heard about the importance of making funeral pre-arrangements, I never did it for myself or Louise. One never realizes how many disturbing and sensitive details are involved in this endeavor until one has to do it. There are the multi-levels of governments to deal with, the insurance companies, the banks, the will, the lawyers, etc., etc. The list is endless. Even though the act of accomplishing these tasks is emotionally draining and difficult, it nevertheless helps me to block out the early debilitating throes of grief, something I am very grateful for.

With cold, emotionless and detached rationality, a fact that will surprise me later on when I'll think back about this, I focus on the most pressing tasks at hand, and I embark on a journey that will drag me through the most frantic period of my life. I feel I have no choice to do this now while I am still in a state of shock, for later on, when the much-needed adrenaline stops pumping in my veins, it will be too late. With the sense of urgency and the need to run away gone, I will once more retreat into myself, feel the pain again and fall back into the paralyzing grips of grief.

December 7, 2010; one week later

A time of intense grief and recollection

I will not enumerate exhaustively what I did during that frenzied period, though I would like to share with you the most ripping task I had to achieve: the disposal of Louise's personal effects. There are different schools of thought on this. Some people hang on forever to the personal possessions of their deceased loved ones, never moving a shoe from where it lay when the person died or keeping their dead child's room intact for years. Others are more selective and keep only mementos such as the funeral ashes, specific pieces of jewelry or clothing, special pictures, etc. Others, like me, dispose of everything as soon as possible in an effort to eliminate from view objects that could be a painful reminder of the lost loved one. No one reaction in particular is the right one, but is merely a personal choice on how each person deals with grief.

Clearing out Louise's wardrobe

Its 4:30 a.m. and I can't sleep again. I have had problems sleeping all my life, but more so since I'm alone. I get out of bed, brew the strongest coffee I can find in the house, sit down in my empty kitchen and start sipping my delicious concoction as I ponder on an idea that has been itching at me for a couple of days now: clear out Louise's belongings. Procrastination no longer an option, I breathe in deeply, stand up and, with wobbly legs, climb up the stairs to the second floor, walk directly to the bedroom wardrobe, open up Louise's half of the closet and stare with mock defiance at all the clothes that once were hers. Every pretty dress, classy suit, delicate blouse, pair of pants or shoes speaks to me; tells me a story, and the sight of them makes Louise's absence utterly real. With a shaky hand, I reach in and unhook one of her favorite garments, a soft turquoise silk blouse that she proudly wore so often. As I bring it closer to me, I am inundated by the delightful scent of her perfume still impregnating the garment, L'Air du

Temps, a fragrance that she wore so well it's as if it was created especially for her. This moment breaks my resolve and I cannot hold back my tears as I lovingly brush the delicate fabric of her blouse across my face, losing myself in her soothing scent one more time.

The process of clearing up Louise's belongings seems excruciatingly long and painful. Tears roll down my cheeks every time I pack one more piece of clothing into the green bags intended for the goodwill store. It's as if I'm saying goodbye to her all over again. Towards the end though, this exercise of parting from her possessions helps me to disconnect and I desensitize a bit. The pain subsides progressively and I thankfully feel a bit freer from the sting of loss, for now at least.

I pack the car with the items for donation and set off for the goodwill store with the intention of taking a long car ride afterwards. Slowly riding in my vehicle with windows open and listening to music has always been my favorite means of escape.

After dropping off Louise's clothes, as planned, I set out for a long car drive hoping it will ease my soul. With windows partly opened and ignoring the cold winter wind blowing through my thinning hair, I succumb to the mellow and soothing melodies playing on the radio. As I start to relax, I fall into some kind of conscious meditative state and I start to reminisce. Images of Louise at various epochs of our lives begin to resurface; I see her in a store smiling and happy, buying her favorite blouse; in a cozy little souvenir shop in Maine while on vacation as she picks out a beautiful black pearl necklace; on the boardwalk in Wildwood City Beach when, while standing, she completely leaned forward and, with her head upside down, peeking through her legs, made funny faces at me. I can still hear her voice as she would, for no reason at all, call out to me and say with exuberance and joy, "Hi my beautiful 'Puppy', I love you" and kiss me gently on the cheek. She was always goofing around in order to make me laugh. We meant everything to each other, we were like one and I miss that so much now.

I remember how she could laugh at herself in the most unusual of situations. One day, while on our honeymoon as we walked on the St Petersburg's beach in Florida, she got curious about a bizarre-looking clam buried in the sand, and bending forward to investigate further, she got spat in the face by the scared clam when it closed up suddenly. What a blast that was! Another time at Upper Canada Village, when feeding the geese a freshly baked loaf of bread we had just bought at the resort store, she had to jump up on a picnic table, screaming and laughing, in order to escape the hungry beaks of the darn geese, who, getting aggressive in their quest for food, started to attack her. Everyone at the scene found this unexpected incident very funny and we laughed a lot.

Why am I not laughing now? Why is it that the more I reminisce, the more painful it gets? Why can't I just let go and enjoy these good moments? Little did I know then that it was just the beginning and that much more sorrow was yet to come.

What's the point of living?

Anger and depression

Overwhelmed with emotions, I pull to the side of the road and let it all out. Man, it seems that all I can do is cry these days. There never seems to be an end to these damn tears. What kind of a wimp am I? The pain, the pain, the freaking pain that bites into me like the closed jaws of a pitbull, when will it let go? Why can't I just run away and leave it all behind? I want to escape so damn bad. I so do not want this hogwash. It is forced upon me and I resent every damn minute of it. God, I hate you with a vengeance. Louise is gone, gone forever. You took her away from me. Now I am nothing but a lost soul pouring its heart out in an empty car by the side of a lonely road. I hurt so bad I just want to die. It would be so easy to drive my car off of a cliff and end it all. I guess it's a question of what hurts more, and right now living is insufferable. It's so tempting, it could be so quick; *finis* with the unbearable pain and sadness; *adios muchachos*, see you in the next life; 'goodbye cruel world,' I'm getting off. But as attractive as offing myself is, I eventually give in to the last ounce of good sense left in me, take a couple of deep breaths and reluctantly pull my car back on the road and set out to face the day once more.

But the reminiscing is not finished yet; in fact it has just begun, and, like a movie playing in my head, the long series of events of my wild ride begins to unravel and I flash back in time.

Chapter 2

Pre-Loss:
The beginning of a long journey into darkness
Shock, denial and anger

January 10, 2008

I was in the gynecologist's office at the Hawkesbury General Hospital, sitting uncomfortably on a straight chair with my back to the wall while the doctor was examining Louise, and I could not help but wonder how fast the events leading us to this office had unraveled. It seemed like only yesterday that our GP, trying unsuccessfully to conceal the concern in his voice, had told us, after examining Louise's hard and swollen stomach, to have a CT scan and blood work done as soon as possible.

I remember the mounting trepidation I felt as I rushed to make the last-minute appointments with medical labs as most of them were closed for the New Year holiday, and the impatience and foreboding creeping up on me as I sat in the hallway of the medical center I had scrounged to find, waiting for the CT scan results. "It's going to be all right," I repeated to myself over and over again as I tried to create hopeful scenarios with a more benign outcome than the dreaded 'C' word. However, my worst fears materialized when I learned from the radiologist that the scan showed two large anomalies on Louise's ovaries. "There's no way to tell if the tumors are cancerous yet," he said in an effort to ease our obvious apprehension. *I guess there's still hope*, I thought, although the sentence "possible ovarian carcinoma" I read on his report sounded pretty damn scary and heavily suggestive of cancer. At that particular moment, my thoughts went to Louise, and how she must have felt to be the main rider in that roller-coaster ride of dread and hope. *What a bum rap*, I thought with sadness.

Suddenly a rustling of paper brought me back out of my reverie and I focused back on the reality of the moment. The gynecologist was methodically washing his hands as Louise, handicapped by her swollen tummy, was struggling to sit up straight on the examining table. Why didn't I help her up from the bed? I criticize myself now as I write these lines. I guess I must have been too caught up in my own selfish concerns to react appropriately. Nevertheless, I feel guilty now and I must learn to deal with that. Oh man! Why did this have to happen?

The events that were about to unravel will forever be imprinted in my mind; sitting straight and rigid with uneasy expectation, I heard what to me at least sounded like the loud and resounding voice of the Devil: "Mrs Milot, I'm afraid you may have ovarian cancer..." What? Did I hear right? What a shock! I was electrified and I was certain that if the chair on which I was sitting would not have been resting against the wall, I would have keeled over. With my mouth wide open in shock and astonishment, like in the famous Canadian Cancer Society television commercial, I would have fallen backwards, knocking my head on the cold, hard floor. It's impossible. This bozo must be wrong; he doesn't know what the hell he's talking about; we need a second opinion. More doctors, more tests, and fast.

More anger!

What also put me off was how offhandedly the doctor treated the whole situation. After coldly announcing the devastating news to Louise, he turned around towards his nursing assistant, asked for a paper tissue and with the most casual and uncaring attitude passed it along to Louise, who at that time had become very disturbed and was sobbing miserably. I could just have strangled the bastard. Couldn't he have shown a little bit more compassion and humanity? I know it's a dirty job and that somebody's got to do it, but still, put up a façade or something, man. Why not be a little more hypocritical and try to show that you care, at least a little bit?

After this devastating and shocking moment, we left the doctor's office with a reference to consult with the Ottawa General Hospital's team of gyn-oncologists, which was not a good omen. We were to make the call to book an appointment with a specialist as soon as possible. "It's urgent," the doctor had said. *Oh boy*, I thought, *this is it, this is the big one.* In a discombobulated state, trying somehow to reassure Louise with a fake smile and a false laid-back attitude, I said: "It will be all right, sweetie, you'll see," and we made our way to the car for the trip back home. What an empty promise that was if I ever made one.

In the days that followed, my time, aside from reassuring Louise and doing all I could to remain calm, was spent trying to make sense out of the horrendous reality of the moment. I spent countless hours researching the internet on diseases and conditions that could be the cause of Louise's predicament. I did not want to accept the fact that it could be cancer and that I could lose her, but still, a sickening sense of dread was creeping in slowly, telling me otherwise. The very thought of the cancer scenario made my head spin as if I were in a drunken stupor and left me speechless. Even though the possibility of cancer was not confirmed yet, there would be at least major surgery in her tummy, and that was scary.

The days painfully became weeks and finally the so-awaited phone call came: we were to meet with a specialist from the gyn-oncologist's team at the Ottawa Hospital's Riverside Campus on February 5th for an evaluation and prep talk for the surgery. Following that call I entered into panic mode and my mind went into overdrive. Suddenly, a cocktail of feelings of relief, hope, dread, fear and disbelief intermingled in my head in a huge mental traffic jam. I felt trapped, cornered in a place I never thought I would be. *This could never happen to me*, I had thought when I would occasionally hear of others caught up in similar situations. Somehow, because Louise and I always took good care of ourselves—nutrition, exercise, mental hygiene, etc.—I believed that we were somehow immune from this kind of thing. I was stunned, shocked and angry all at once. Depression and helplessness were also at the *rendezvous*. What's the point of maintaining a healthy lifestyle if it leads to this? My determination at winning this coming battle was weakening by the minute. I wanted to be anywhere else but in this reality, and at times I lost myself in some kind of 'fantasyland' wishful thinking. Why couldn't Louise and I, like in a *Star Trek* motion picture, hold each other in an endless embrace, and in a magical, sparkling whirlwind disintegrate into a zillion pieces to lose ourselves forever into oblivion, happy and away from all this crap? But unfortunately, we don't live in a movie and soon I was to find out that reality often surpasses fiction.

February 5, 2008

Details of the surgery

The Riverside Campus was fairly easy to find and get to, even though that day was plagued by a snow storm. "Gawd, I hate snow," I bitched as I desperately struggled to find a spot to ditch the car in the overcrowded parking lot. After many attempts and confrontations with other stressed-out poor saps like us, we finally succeeded in squeezing the car into a tight little spot which was probably illegal (didn't care), and we rushed through the front door. With feet still dripping wet with the yucky white stuff, we proceeded hurriedly through a labyrinth of corridors and alleys to finally arrive at our destination, barely making it in time for our appointment.

After only a short wait, which I very much appreciated, we were called into the gyn-oncologist's office. At that point, even though the emotional numbness had set in for some time now, my legs were a little wobbly and my heart was pounding at the anticipation of learning the details on how the surgeon was going to butcher my wife. No other way around it. He explained every little gory detail of the operation to come: complete hysterectomy. Trust me, you have to have a good stomach to be able to sit through this, and even though I always thought of myself as a tough guy, I wasn't so tough now, feeling cornered and scared like a kid in that stuffy little room. A nauseating wave of fear was mounting and I wanted to run away as far and as fast as I could. But my wimpy fleeting moment of weakness soon dissipated when I noticed how Louise stood tall in front of it all, how strong she was. At that instant, my thoughts went to her and I wondered, in spite of her bravado, how it really felt to be at the receiving end of that prickly skewer.

As if the verbal description of the procedure wasn't anguishing enough, our tormentor twisted the hot iron even deeper by methodically showing us detailed graphics of the organs that were to be removed. Great! A lecture in med class could not have been more of a routine for him. Did we really need to know this much? Did he not fathom, even for a tiny little moment, that for us it could represent the end of the world, literally? Maybe I'm asking a little too much here, but what about a little TLC? Maybe Medicine 101 could cover subjects like 'bedside manner and sensitivity', or how about this: 'how not to make your patients want to jump off of a cliff after you give them the bad news'.

After our short crash course on 'how to be disemboweled in three easy steps', which, by the way, completely scared the shit out of us, we were invited to sign the mandatory disclaimer stating that we had been properly informed of the risks involved in the procedure. I'm not entirely sure of this, and I would not swear by it, but I think that somewhere in all of the medical and legal jargon printed on that waiver, we agreed that the Institution and the surgeons involved could not be held responsible for any harm caused to the patient, or at least they could make it difficult for us to sue their asses off. The fact that the medical interveners have a way of sheltering themselves from future negative reper-cussions resulting from their interventions with their patients is a point that impressed me all through my rubbing elbows with medical professionals through this incredible adventure. Does the fear of future lawsuits pending continuously over their heads inhibit their ability to be efficient practitioners? Does this fear hold back doctors from giving the much-needed hope of recovery to a suffering patient in the fear that if things go bad, they could be sued for not holding up such promises? From my perspective at this time, I think it does in many cases.

Half in shock and with our tails between our legs, we left the hospital after being told to expect a call from the administration office for an appointment for the pre-admission and pre-operation tests.

February 15, 2008

Pre-admission

Back at the hospital for the pre-admission, we spent some time filling out a bunch of papers at the administration office and Louise was occupied most of the day going through an endless series of tests to make sure that she was fit to withstand the surgery. Everything went smoothly and fast, a positive point for the hospital.

Nothing of consequence happened that day other than the fact that Louise was still behaving like a trooper, and I was darn proud of her. I wish I could say the same for me though, for I could feel the trepidations of a little storm brewing inside of me at the thought of the dreaded surgery day. Of course I forced myself to keep a straight face and a reassuring attitude. Louise needed all the support and strength I could offer; no wimps allowed in this play. I had no idea then that the words 'strength and resilience' would take on a whole new meaning for me in the months and years to come. I was an unsuspecting player in a game that would take me to levels of extremeness I never thought I was capable of.

Mental note

As I write these lines today I ponder on the importance and the necessity of not knowing the future. Could I have gone on if I would have known how difficult my voyage would be? How about Louise? Would she have given up? Would I have worked as hard if I had known the outcome of my journey? Was the end result already written or did we have a say in it? Was I just a travel companion in Louise's journey, enhancing my own learning through her experience? I guess I will never know the answers to these questions. I tend to believe that we come to this world with a karmic baggage that predestines us to a specific destiny. I also believe that through personal assiduous efforts, we can go beyond that same destiny line and create a new and better reality for ourselves; the future is not necessarily set. On the 'not-so-sure side' though, I think that fate, chance or bad luck may have something to do in our tribulations and that sometimes we just tag along for the ride, learning as best as we can. Who really knows?

February 15, 2008

The wait

We left the hospital somewhat satisfied that the day went smoothly in spite of my little emotional moments and returned home with a list of instructions to prepare for the big day. Again, we were to wait for another phone call from the administration office to book a time and date for the operation. The wait would be both long and short at the same time. On the one hand, I was impatient for the operation to be over, as Louise was suffering, but on the other hand, I was terrified to face the frightful day.

Chapter 3

Post-Loss:
December 10, 2010

Reaction to the separation, pain and feelings of loss
Recollecting the deceased in the relationship

I'm nervously holding the soft grey leather-covered steering wheel of my white 2007 Hyundai as I drive reluctantly through the city of Cornwall. The drive along Pitt Street is a dull one on this somber day. The dark, cloud-covered sky, and the wet snow falling lazily on the pavement, colors the day with more sadness and further enhances my sense of loss.

I see it further ahead, the little building on the right side of the street tucked up against the parking lot of a small shopping mall. My heart makes a double beat as the knife in my gut painfully slices another inch deeper; I want to turn around and chicken out. *Maybe tomorrow will be easier, maybe next week or next month. Ah, God, this is so tough,* I cowardly think as I make a sharp right turn into the driveway, park the car in front of the main entrance, and as I enter, stare defiantly at the institution's logo: Wilson Funeral Home.

A very dignified tall grey-haired gentleman dressed elegantly in the customary white shirt and black suit politely welcomes me inside and I state my business. "I'm here to pick up my late wife's ashes," I say in a shy and contained voice. "Her name is…ah…was Louise Milot." Thinking and talking of Louise in the past tense is somewhat of a challenge for me, and every time I do it, my heart skips a beat.

Completing the paperwork and collecting the urn takes no more than 10 to 15 minutes and I rush out of there presto. As I carry my precious cargo reverently wrapped up in the usual mauve velvet bag, I can't help but notice how heavy it is. With mixed emotions, not sure if I should hold it close to my heart or be afraid of it, I lay the urn delicately on the empty passenger seat, another painful reminder of Louise's absence.

Is this all that's left of her, a pile of ashes? Louise who was once a vibrant, loving and intelligent human being is reduced to this? Damn life, why are you so fragile!

After a few minutes of hesitation, I untie the knot that's keeping the bag closed and, with a trembling hand, I finally dare to softly touch the cold metal. With teary eyes I say goodbye to her one more time.

Louise was a 5 feet 4 inches tall, cute brunette with piercing brown eyes and a disarming smile. She had managed to remain slim and trim for the first years of our marriage, but her gene pool getting the best of her, she had regretfully settled for being pleasantly plump for the rest of her life. A bit of a tomboy at times, she nevertheless exhibited female attributes that did not remain unnoticed. At work, she was the epitome of the efficient executive assistant, capable of multi-tasking like no one else. Always protecting the underdog, she was loved and respected by all her co-workers who often referred to her as 'mother' because of her caring and protective attitude.

Her blazing temperament occasionally flared up, and being at the receiving end of her scowl and verbal disapproval was an experience not to be forgotten. Overall, although a bit of a recluse who cherished her privacy, Louise was a kind, generous and strong person who possessed an inner beauty that left no one indifferent. I miss you, honey!

Coming back home now takes on a whole new meaning and I'm reminded of that as I turn onto the short narrow street leading to my house. Once a cute and cozy Georgian country house with gingerbread trim ornamenting the wrap-around veranda, it is now nothing else but a painful reminder of what my life used to be. Can I ever look at my home again and not have my heart shredded to pieces every time I see the old couch tucked in on the porch where Louise used to sit for hours knitting sweaters for me? Can I ever peek through my second-floor office window and stare at the 'Robin's Nest' corner without remembering sorrowfully the time I built it for her? It was a cute small rest area with a Victorian park bench amid a backdrop of lovely colorful bird-houses. The first time she tried it, she cried and said, "You build beautiful things. Thank you, I love it." How can I erase the pain triggered by the sight of all that was our life together? I'm lost and desperate for relief.

I park the car under the massive maple tree overhanging the driveway and enter the house wondering where I'm going to store the urn until the reunion with family and friends for her celebration of life. The old summer country kitchen is a good place as I don't have to go there often. I unceremoniously place the container on a shelf as if it was burning coals and hurry to the dining room in a desperate attempt to escape the hurt.

A useless gesture; I'm still choking, my throat is still constricted and I feel the walls closing in on me rapidly. Air, I need air! I restlessly tour the house, but every room I visit tells the same story, nothing but loneliness, nothing but pain. I finally give up, get dressed and walk right back out, jump into my car, my only means of escape these days, open the window, turn the radio on and take off to nowhere.

Oh! How I would love to be able to escape this damn pain, this horrible insisting feeling that my gut is being mercilessly shredded to pieces by some invisible hand. The hurt, the hurt, at times I can barely stand it, and at this precise moment I would do anything to make it disappear. Anything!

But as usual, my faithful and reliable friend does the trick again for me, and as I drive along the spiraling road by the side of the St Lawrence River, I can slowly breathe again. I feel a little bit more in control and able to pull myself together, even though my momentary reprieve is constantly interrupted by a sudden urge to rush back home to take care of Louise. Being my wife's sole care-provider is all that I have been doing for the last three years and I feel that only time will allow me to free myself from this conditioning. I quickly come back to the moment though, as I realize that the object of my compulsion is not there anymore, home is but an empty house, Louise is gone and I have all the time in the world now.

Those are questions I keep asking myself these days, though. Where could I go? What could I do? Sell the house and move into a small condo in the next town? Sell everything I own and move to another province, another country and start a new life? How about Florida where it's nice and warm? Here is something I always wanted to do; why not now? I have nothing to lose, for I have lost everything anyway. This goes on and on for days, weeks; I concoct every possible scenario which would allow me to run, escape reality and leave the pain behind, if that's ever possible. But in the end, I give in to that damn little inner voice again and let reason set in; I decide to stick around a bit longer. Why though, I don't know yet and I sincerely hope that in the future I will gain from this decision.

During the years that Louise was sick, I devoured countless books on grieving and they were all adamant about one thing: do not make any important decision within at least one year of the loss. So, with that in mind, moving or selling the house was not an option.

In the equation there was also my old dog Max to consider. Max is an adorable 12-year-old black cocker spaniel with irresistible imploring brown eyes, long floppy ears and soft shiny velvety hair. He always required lots of TLC because of his vulnerability to ear and eye infections, which rendered him even more endearing to me. From the start, to my chagrin, he was always Louise's dog and stayed mostly by her side, even more so when she was sick, as if he knew something was wrong. When she passed, he endlessly searched the house looking for her, would not play, ate very little and eventually entered into a state of permanent passivity; he was never the same again. It broke my heart to see him like this and I could not allow my own selfishness to perturb his life any further by suddenly changing his environment. Not to mention that I also felt uneasy and guilty about leaving him alone for long periods of time even though I had to from time to time. I figured he'd been neglected enough through Louise's sickness and that he deserved more attention now. In the end, he became the main reason why I did not sell the house and why I decided to stay and face the music. Will I question this decision in the months to come? Only time will tell.

December 12, 2010

Reunion for the celebration of Louise's life

Its 11 a.m. and the drive from Martintown to St Andrews West is a long and arduous one. The uneasiness I feel keeps me from appreciating the beauty of County Road 18; a scenic road bursting with beautifully manicured farms set on a bed of relaxing rolling hills. Normally, even winter cannot tarnish this image, but today my head is wrapped up in a cloud of fear and apprehension and I can only think of one thing: facing family and friends for Louise's celebration of life.

Of the 40 people I have invited to the reunion, only 12 of them confirmed their presence, as the damn weatherman predicted a massive snow storm that scared everyone away. Right now, I'm driving with my windshield wipers working full blast as it is not snow falling, but a torrent of rain. *They could have come anyway*, I think in frustration, sad that Louise will not get the send-off that she deserves.

I drive a little further and arrive at the Quinn's Inn, a turn-of-the-century superb old stone house that once was the Ontario Governor's residence. I exit my parked car and set out to enter the Inn as I clutch Louise's urn nervously. I take a deep breath, climb up the old worn-out wooden stairs and enter the main dining room. There they all are; I see them all bunched up in a cozy corner by the massive blazing fireplace. They all turn their heads and watch me as I approach with uncertain steps to deposit Louise's urn and photo on the large window sill behind the long table where they all sit. Exhibiting a feeble smile and trying to look as casual as I can, I collapse on the first chair I can find and salute everyone. They all respond in kind, and the conversation starts to flow. One by one, people stand up and walk in front of Louise's picture to pay their respect and reminisce. Aside from the occasional tear, there are no uncomfortable wailing moments and I even see a few smiles. What a bunch of troopers. Surprisingly enough, aside from a few chest stabs, I'm holding on very well and the morning goes on better than expected. Family members and friends, each in their own way, are polite and protective of me, something I appreciate, for in spite of my fake debonair attitude, I feel I could break at any moment and do not know how long I can continue with this masquerade. The Inn's buffet is succulent as usual and, ironically, everyone seems to be enjoying themselves.

Outside in the wet parking lot when the reunion is over, after the usual hugs, kisses, handshakes and empty promises to see each other soon, we part and everyone goes home. As I drive back to my empty house, I can't help but be amazed at most people's resilience in the face of adversity and how they are able to carry on in spite of this tragic moment. Although, stubbornly holding on to my desire to face this alone, I am doubtful of my own resilience and decide to solicit the help of an old friend. Back at home, I enter the kitchen, open the cupboard door and reach for a bottle of Glenfiddich!

Chapter 4

Pre-Loss:
February 22, 2008
Experiencing deep emotions: sadness, anger, guilt and shame

The dreaded surgery day

With a heavy heart I had taken Max to the dog kindergarten the day before. I always hated to leave him behind and I'm sure that, through some kind of canine wisdom, he knew this, for he certainly made every effort to look miserable and abandoned in the hopes I would change my mind. Thus, in an effort to minimize my guilt, I suckered up and booked him a room with a view, the most expensive dog condo available at the kennel.

The dreaded moment finally arrived and after religiously following the pre-op instructions, we departed for the hospital. Once there, we were directed to the surgery room's sitting area where Louise was prompted to don the customary hospital gown. For some unknown reason, she also had to wear these long tight white stockings that looked downright uncomfortable, and they were as it turned out, according to Louise. She had been fasting since the night before and looked pale and feeble. The operation was scheduled for 1 p.m. but we were asked to arrive at 11 a.m. The wait would be long and I was concerned that Louise would collapse out of weakness. The chairs in the waiting room, which we shared with what looked like a million other people, felt hard and uncomfortable. Once in a while the name of a patient would be called out and a woman would disappear through a door into a mysterious room to the left. After some time, accompanied by an orderly, she would reappear and would be rolled out of there lying on a gurney *en route* to one of the surgery rooms. Resigned to an uncertain fate, the patients all had that same kind of worried and anxious look.

This went on for over two hours and Louise was starting to show serious signs of fatigue. Without nourishment for the past 18 hours, she was very weak, dizzy, and nauseous and was seeing kaleidoscopes. By that time, the waiting room had cleared up a bit and I made her lie on her side on two chairs. Needless to say, I was on the verge of making a scene when finally her name was called out. Never in my life will I be able to erase the painful sight of watching her stumbling along on shaky legs and barely making it to the famous prep room door.

Again, one more time as I write these lines, I shamefully ask myself why I did not disobey the hospital's strict directives and escort and support her into that damn room. Anyway, after what seemed to be like an eternity, she was finally rolled out on a gurney, and as she passed in front of me, she smiled softly, trying unsuccessfully to hide her worried eyes. I stared at the gurney as far as I could see it, and when the door to the operation room finally closed on her, a horrible sense of dread overcame me as I realized that I might never see her alive again. The protective numbness that had been engulfing me for a while now instantly dissipated and I was massively overwhelmed by a sense of trepidation that would not leave me for days to come.

Three hours passed and I was impatiently walking back and forth in the corridor adjacent to the recovery room when all of a sudden an orderly walked towards me and announced that the surgeon was coming soon to debrief me on how the operation went. After waiting a while, as I stared around with anxiety I saw her at the end of a corridor walking towards me. She was a tiny little blue-eyed woman with short blonde hair and she was still dressed up in her blue-green work garment that was still stained with barely noticeable tiny little specs of Louise's blood. She obviously had rushed out of the operating room, not noticing the stains I am sure, and had lost no time to graciously come talk with me, a gesture I appreciated.

"Mr Milot?" she called out. "I'm Dr A. Would you come into the office so that we can talk?" It was a directive more than a question but I didn't care and although I was terrified to know the truth, I was ecstatic at the same time to know that my apprehensions would soon be alleviated. "What were you told regarding your wife's condition?" she asked. You see, up until that moment, it was not clear that Louise's tumors where cancerous. Only after opening her up would they know. They knew now. It was cancer, and the news hit me like a ton of bricks even though I had suspected it for a while. "The hysterectomy was a success but I cannot be certain to have been able to remove all the other tiny little tumors logged in the surrounding tissues, but I did my best and chemotherapy should do the rest," she said. "She is OK for now and you can see her soon." The little innuendos 'should' and 'for now' in her sentences did not pass by me unnoticed. It sort of implied subtly that she might not be OK later on and it made me feel even more insecure. I would have to face this kind of 'mumbo jumbo' talk all through our dealings with doctors at the hospital; never giving us complete hope and always keeping us in doubt of success.

It had now been five hours since the operation began and two hours since I saw the doctor. I was pacing like a caged lion in the corridor waiting to see Louise. No one was telling me anything and I was in total darkness as to whether Louise was half-dead or alive. Slowly becoming a source of frustration to me was a woman sitting at a desk by the door, evidently controlling all traffic to the recovery room. Every attempt I made to fish for information was coldly rebuked by her and I was told to wait again and again. My patience was challenged to its limits, I felt helpless and overwhelmed with worries when all of a sudden, I was given the so-awaited signal: "You can go in now, Mr Milot!" Not waiting to be told a second time, I hurried through the infamous door and apprehensively entered the up-to-now forbidden room.

As I walked in, the sight that was offered to me was disturbing to say the least and I was assaulted by a few painful stabs in the solar plexus. My ears were overwhelmed by a cacophony of annoying beeping sounds while my eyes distressingly saw nothing else but rows and rows of white-sheeted beds with feeble-looking patients lying on them. The hard fact that they were all wired up and connected to intimidating-looking bleeping apparatus made the scene even more morbid. Blood and needles always gave me the jitters, I just can't help it.

I walked with trepidation through the long room, almost running one minute and crawling like a turtle the next. The joy of seeing Louise was ruined by the paralyzing apprehension of the almost certain unbearable pain I would feel at the sight of her all cut up and patched up, like the subject of an experiment gone wrong. After an excruciating lengthy walk through this chamber of horror, I finally made it to Louise's bed, but before I even had the chance to take a furtive look, I heard the nurse saying to me, "She is still very groggy. The operation was long and difficult and we had to drug her up pretty heavily…We almost lost her, you know," she said again. "Please be brief and let her rest, she needs it badly." Great, thanks, just what I needed to hear; why don't you just shoot me and end it right now while you're at it?

So, with increased apprehension, I turned around towards the bed and finally dared to take a look at my sweet baby. My heart took a double beat and I was immediately overwhelmed by a wave of sadness at seeing her like this. Even though she was comfortably covered with sparkling white sheets, I could still see her exposed limp arm lying on the side of the bed giving way to her delicate hand, its thin skin pierced by a needle, and I flinched. A clear plastic bag was hooked up on a stand overhanging her bed and a thick liquid slowly dripped into the needle, feeding her weak body. Her face was pale and she looked exhausted, but nevertheless, sensing my presence, she made an effort to gaze lazily at me and said with a barely audible voice: "How are you?"

Shocked at hearing her words, I nearly collapsed on a chair by the bed. Imagine, even all cut up, drugged up and under the very serious threat of dying, the first thought she had was filled with concerns for me. "I'm all right, honey," I repeated over and over again. "Rest. You did beautifully, I am very proud of you," I told her softly. At that moment, I realized how much I loved her and how precious she was to me. For the first time in my life, I was witnessing true unselfish love, and I felt blessed to be at the receiving end of that love. I was overwhelmed with joy and I was honored to share my life with such a wonderful human being.

I did not stay very long for fear of tiring her, and after exchanging a few ushered words, reassured that she was comfortable, pain-free and in good hands, I left and drove to my hotel nearby. I had to rest for what I suspected was going to be a long and bumpy ride, but I knew that sleep would not come easily. In anticipation of this, I came equipped with the necessary assistants: sleeping pills and Scotch.

I always hated to be in a hotel room by myself, and this time was no different. It was worse even, much worse. The room felt enormously big, bare and empty. My chest hurt and my stomach was in a churn. As soon as I could, I popped two sleeping pills, filled the traditional clear plastic hotel glass to the brim, not even bothering with ice, and took a big swig. I could feel the satisfying liquid burning its way down my pipes *en route* to my stomach as I collapsed on the bed in front of the television, hoping to escape my torments as soon as possible. After gulping down the rest of my booze, I progressively slipped into oblivion, slept like a log and woke up surprisingly clear-headed the next morning. All fired up under the influence of a rush of adrenaline, I was ready to face the new day ahead and whatever challenges it might bring. At the same time, I was also very anxious to see Louise again, wondering what kind of shape she would be in.

The drive to the hospital was short, with surprisingly little traffic. After entering the hospital, I went to the patient information desk to be directed to the new room she had been moved to during the night. As I entered the area, I was pleasantly surprised to see Louise propped up in her bed, wide awake, welcoming me with a big happy smile. I smiled back, and barely able to contain my relief and joy at seeing her like this, I said excitedly, "Hi honey, how are you today?" We started to chat and it went on from there.

The hours and days somehow passed by quickly as the routine tests and exams were continually performed. From time to time an important-looking doctor with pen in hand and carrying a bunch of medical files would come by for a visit to monitor Louise's progress. The usual feelings of insecurity and anxiety were at the party, but the professional and patient attitude of the nursing staff helped us to somehow cope better with these difficult circumstances. Aside from a few bumps and scary moments, the events were unfolding as they should and Louise was making the expected hoped-for progress.

Her targeted release date from the hospital was rapidly approaching and we could not wait to get out of that place. But there were a few hurdles to jump before we got there as we would soon learn. For instance, the importance of not removing her bladder shunt too soon, otherwise it would have to be reinserted a second time as it was a painful procedure when done after the surgery. The other major source of concern was the evacuation of gases and fecal matter. This was a biggy for Louise as she always had been chronically constipated. The farting part was not a problem for her, or so she thought, and she was surprised to learn that the massive amount of medication ingested in the past week had blocked her pipes and had rendered her kind of 'silent' and 'tight ass,' so to speak. "Never mind the hard stuff," she said to me, "that will come later. For now, let's get some wind going."

The solution to counter this problem according to the nurses was to walk endlessly in order to stimulate the peristaltic movement and get the bowels moving again. So, enriched with that knowledge, Louise, looking a little funny dressed in the traditional hospital gown and hooked up to her mobile serum stand, proceeded to endlessly haunt the hospital corridors in the hopes that the gas factory would soon open its doors again. As for me, like a faithful puppy, I accompanied her around and around the eighth floor of the hospital's convoluted passageways, smiling and discreetly waving here and there at the oncoming walking patients, wondering in amusement if they needed to fart too. While Louise was in a continuous struggle to keep her naked *derrière* from showing through the rear opening of her hospital gown, I, on the other hand, was on constant alert for any possible sound coming out of her butt cheeks. Nothing, not a damn sound, and as disheartening as it may have been, we bravely kept up the scenario.

Eventually one day, when returning to her room, completely exhausted and discouraged, she felt the urge to 'go.' She had been in the bathroom for a few minutes and I had just flopped into a chair when, all of a sudden, I heard a resounding and surprisingly loud noise behind the door. No explanation necessary, I understood what had just happened, and when Louise poked her smiling mug through the opened door, everyone in the room applauded. What a great moment that was!

The second phase of the 'evac.' operation went smoothly and the hopes of escaping our bad dream just increased by a couple of notches.

While waiting for Louise's release from the hospital, another scrumptious little moment worth mentioning occurred.

Since her arrival at the hospital, Louise had been waiting to enjoy the private room she had been promised, but so far, the only ones available were double-bed units. After some time had passed, a nurse finally entered the room and announced proudly that a private room had just been freed up for Louise and that she could move in immediately. "Great news!" I blurted.

Furthermore, she told me that I could sleep beside Louise on a cot that she would bring in later on. So, all excited, I rushed out of the hospital to gladly dispose of my depressing hotel room. Little did I know then that the night to come would be nightmarish and full of surprises.

Back at the hospital, savoring my newfound privacy and lounging comfortably in a high-back chair for just a short while, I noticed the same nurse diligently enter the room with a disturbed look on her face: There had been a massive car accident with multiple injuries and they needed the room because it contained special equipment that was needed for the treatment of some of the wounded. So, not only were we kicked out of the room without reverence, Louise was swiftly moved into a four-bed area, which was definitely a downer. She was put off big time, but sympathized nevertheless with those poor people who needed urgent help.

So that's what all the sirens were all about when I was coming back from the hotel, I thought, and I started to freak out as a scary thought popped into my mind: *Where the heck am I going to sleep tonight?* Certainly not in that cramped and noisy chamber of doom filled with moaning and snoring people. There was just not enough space for me. Louise was demoralized, and I was not far behind, but my weariness was rapidly appeased when the nurse, noticing the panicked look on my disenchanted mug, came to my rescue and said that she would set me up for the night with a portable bed in the patients' courtesy room. It would be quiet in there for the night, but she explained I'd have to rise up early and get out at 6 a.m., before it opened up again. Well, that was not the highlight of my day, but it would have to do, since I could not check back into my hotel room. There was a convention in town and the surrounding hotels were all booked up.

So, here I went, holding sheets and pillow, *en route* to my improvised bedroom. Mumbling all the way my dissatisfaction, I set the sheets up on the cot, closed the door, put out the lights and proceeded to lie on my bed of fortune. Try to imagine this ridiculous scene: I'm a 5 feet 11 inches tall adult and the cot was one of those folding beds that must have been made to accommodate a small child. It was a joke. When I sat my butt in the middle of the mattress and stretched, my feet hung out of the end of the bed by about 1 foot and my head stuck out in empty space like a scary puppet. The only way I could fit in was in some kind of fetal position or on my back, legs bent upwards. Any position I tried to contort myself into was unbearable and the night was going to be long, very long. Little did I know also that this little inconvenience was nothing compared to the heart-stopping shock that was about to scare the crap out of me.

It was about 3 a.m. and after tossing and turning like a wiggling worm, I finally fell asleep and slipped into a light dream state. My reverie was short-lived though as I was slowly awakened by a soft shuffling sound and became progressively aware of a presence near me.

Still in a sleepy haze, I hesitantly turned around to investigate the disturbance. I just could not believe what my inquisitive eyes were seeing. With mounting trepidation, as my vision was slowly adapting to the darkness of the room, I was beginning to see the outline of a misty shadow taking shape. My skin was crawling as if an army of ants was invading my whole body and my pounding heart was menacing to burst through my chest as the ghostly image was becoming more and more defined. Barely able to contain myself and in a panic, I clumsily tried to throw my sorry ass out of that stupid bed, but my rickety legs, numbed from being contorted all that time, could not hold me and, like a sack of sand, I collapsed to the floor ready to scream like a scared puppy. Terrorized, I could not keep myself from staring at the invader, when all of a sudden the mysterious enigma was solved: it was Louise, who with head and shoulders covered by a white sheet, was sitting in a chair quietly observing me sleeping.

The words that came out of my mouth at this moment were

not very nice and this instance was the only time that I ever spoke to her this way: "What the f— are you doing? I almost died of a heart attack. What the hell were you thinking, for Christ's sake?" Luckily, she did not take offence to my bum rhetoric and, thinking that the whole adventure was hilarious, she almost rolled on the floor laughing. What had happened was that Louise, totally frustrated at not being able to sleep because of all the racket in that room, had covered herself up with a bed sheet to keep warm and had stormed out of her room. Out of concern for me, she had walked into the patient lounge to see how I was doing. Later, in answer to my somewhat abrupt question: "Why the hell did you not tell me it was you?" she answered patiently, "I didn't want to wake you up, so I just sat there and watched you sleep, that's all."

Later on when I regained my bearings and my hands stopped shaking, I somehow managed to see the humor in the whole thing and started laughing too. If you can't laugh at yourself, who can you laugh at? I will never forget that little episode. That was one for the books.

Needless to say, we did not sleep much that night, Louise lying on the couch and me curled up like a pretzel on that awful contraption. When finally morning came, we rushed back to the room just in time to meet the oncologist as he was doing his usual morning rounds. When he entered the room though, he visited Louise's neighbor's bed just long enough to coldly mutter to her a few 'not so' encouraging words such as, "I'm afraid, Mrs S., that our last efforts to treat your cancer have failed and that we cannot do anything more for you. We will have a talk with your husband to make the necessary arrangements." We did not wait (or want) to hear the sobbing sounds that were about to come out of that poor soul later on. We unfortunately couldn't afford to even care about that lady as we were ourselves too caught up in our own little world in fear of dancing to the same tune. But thankfully it was not to be and Louise got her release. All excited and impatient to leave, she listened distractedly to the usual post-op recommendations, dressed up at lightning speed, said goodbye to the nurses on duty, and we rushed out of the hospital like a couple of bats out of hell, hoping that our problems were over. Think again, Sam!

Chapter 5

Post-Loss:
January 10, 2011

*Experiencing deep pain, frustration, resentment and great
feelings of loss
Learning to let go of the pain and sadness associated with
the old attachments
Developing positive coping strategies*

It's 12 noon and I feel a strong urge to get drunk again. It has been
my pattern for the past weeks now, uselessly messing around on
the computer, tying up loose ends all morning and drinking
Scotch at midday. The intoxicating liquid always helps me to
escape the dark grips of grief that resurface the very minute I
attempt to relax my mind. No wonder I like it so much! As hard
as I try, I can only manage to stay pain-free for a couple of hours
at a time and again and again I need support from 'Glenfiddich,'
my best friend and favorite single-malt Scotch. But every time the
numbing effect of the alcohol dissipates, the painful reality shows
its ugly head again and I sink once more into darkness. When
that happens, I suffocate and I need air, lots of it. Every single
time it's the same: run out to escape the confines of my prison,
ignore any ounce of logic I may have, and, still boozed up significantly, jump into my car and take off for a long ride by the river,
my second-best mean of escape at this point.

Driving under the influence has always been against my
principles and I feel guilty every time I do it, but the pain is so
unbearable that I can't help myself. Day after day it's the same
scenario and even the few close calls I have by narrowly escaping
police barrages do not deter me from my recklessness. I am so
miserable and out of it at times that I don't even care if I lose my
driver's license, or get into an accident and hurt someone. Grief

is a horrible thing; it changes people and it surely has brought up the worst in me at times.

One day though, in a flash of common sense, I decide to take a plunge and call the police to inquire about the legal blood/alcohol level allowed while driving a vehicle. I also want to know where I can get a breathalyzer to monitor my own level of intoxication. Thus I could at least get my fit and ride without getting into trouble. I was shocked to find out from the police officer on duty that it was only .05. *Crap*, I think, *not even enough to wet my palate, let alone get a buzz*. What a let-down. Sorry I asked! Disappointed, but still determined to do the right thing, I reluctantly decide to find some other means of support to help me get through the days. Although getting stoned at noon has become the highlight of my day, this behavior is nevertheless non-acceptable and is also not the greatest for my health, so I decide to kick my butt and cut down on the boozing.

Ya, right. Wow. What an insight of wisdom. What an empty promise if I ever made one and I wonder how long my newfound maturity will last. That remained to be seen.

Well, it didn't, and, as I had sadly suspected, rebellious Pierre rears his ugly head again and decides that at this stage of the game, abstinence is not an option. *I enjoy drinking and I'll keep on drinking, screw it*, I think with bravado. *I just have to limit my intake (a bit) and hope I don't run into trouble.*

After painfully witnessing Louise dying of freaking cancer in spite of doing everything that was humanly possible to do to be healthy, I've lost faith in life. I am pissed off and frustrated at the sight of brutal gangsters and grossly fat and reckless individuals living to be 90 years old decrepit, while caring and beautiful young souls are savagely taken away from this world. What's the point of taking care of oneself if it doesn't even make a damn difference? Hardship will happen regardless of what one does. *Que sera sera* as the song says. *Whatever will be will be, and I'll die when I die, screw it*, I scream mentally. *To hell with the world, I don't give a damn anymore.*

But eventually my frustrated egotistical whining comes to an end, for now at least, and logic finally kicks in along with the fear of ending up in the slammer, and I make one more deal with myself to ease up on the sauce; although a step in the right direction, it is not nearly enough. I need to sharpen up on my coping strategy.

But for now at least, it feels good to have my private little moments of bitching when I can unleash my frustrations in private without looking like an imbecile. This process also helps me to realize how much anger and sadness is still bottled up inside of my heavy chest and how much more venting I need to do. While wailing and swearing may be liberating and acceptable at times in my grieving process, I don't perceive them as viable options in the long run. I can't let this develop into a permanent behavioral pattern; it's undignified. Of course this kind of thinking leads me to ask the inevitable questions: What are my options? What can I do to pull myself out of this mess and stand up proudly again?

Having had some success at writing articles in the past, I feel that putting words down on paper would be an ideal way to fill my newly found free time and allow my bitching to serve a useful purpose.

Another option is music. I am a musician and playing the piano could be a powerful outlet, but since tickling my black and whites seems to bring out more pain than relief, I'd better forget it for the moment. I decide learning to cope by developing my writing skills seems to be a more appropriate short-term objective, but at this stage of the game I need relief, and fast. I badly need to disconnect myself from the pains of loss if I want to embrace life as it should be. I need to be able to face life in terms of 'I' instead of 'we'. I am single now, 'we' doesn't exist anymore, and although facing the hardships of life by myself is excruciatingly difficult, I need to become 'whole' again.

Having been a trained psychotherapist, martial artist and Zen practitioner for years, I have learned to develop efficient methods to overcome and cope with these kinds of predicaments. I know they are efficient, for I have used them successfully for years with clients. But up to now, I had been too stunned and too numbed by grief to even consider applying them on myself. That will have to change.

'Time is the best healer,' the wise elders claim, and I believe it's true, in my case at least, as my grief matures. I can sense it now, as I crawl through my screeching voyage, a subtle transformation occurring while the constant battle between bad days and good days goes on. Progressively, I experience the occasional pain-free day and savor brief instances of relief when I feel whole again…before the darkness returns.

I want to share with you an article that I wrote on one of those special days. It was meant as a catharsis for me at first, but it made me feel so good that I decided to share it with all my internet friends. By doing this, I was hoping that it might connect with other grievers like me and thus help them overcome their sense of loss: boom, instant success. Within a week I was receiving support e-mails from people all over the world congratulating me on how helpful and soothing my short article was to them. They had a strong connection with me and did not feel alone in their journey. It gave them hope of brighter days to come and helped them see a light at the end of the tunnel, they claimed.

A Good Day in the Life of a Grieving Widower
by Dr Pierre Milot

Strangely enough, today is a good day, it's been so long since I've had one.

All bundled up in my red checkered construction shirt, and discreetly trespassing on my neighbor's long country driveway, I'm taking my old dog Max out for his morning walk. Protected from the cool river wind by the bordering woods, I can feel the hot spring sun gently warming my face and shoulders, and can hear nothing else but the birds chirping, the familiar honking sound of the Canadian wild geese flying high in the clear blue sky happy to come back home, and the delightful crunching sound of gravel underneath my feet as I walk. With an uncertain smile I breathe in the fresh morning breeze, I feel good.

Strolling along, lost in thought, I marvel at our capacity to recover from what seems at times like the 'unrecoverable'. How can it be that today I can smile when only yesterday I was in the deepest of sorrows, with little hope for tomorrow. As I ponder on this, I reminisce, I think back on that dreadful November day, when, as I was holding my wife's cold dying hand and counting her last breaths, she left me in so much pain and loneliness. I remember that while I was putting on a brave front reassuring her that I would be OK, I was prompting her to go towards the 'light' (as if she wasn't already there, for where else could such a kind and loving soul be, but in the arms of an angel).

Little did I know then that very soon I would be kneeling on the ground, bent over in gut-wrenching agony, sobbing like a child, and begging for her to come back. I would have done everything then, change my religion, give away all that I owned, even my life and soul to see and feel her, to be able to one last time delicately run my fingers through her soft silky hair, as I lovingly kiss her forehead while savoring her particular body scent that I've grown to love so much.

But, if the Divine Intelligence in its infinite wisdom has granted us the gift of growth through sorrow and pain, it has also given us the necessary strength to overcome the same hardships. So, reaching inside the deepest confines of my being for that slippery strength, I managed to somehow make the pain more bearable, stand up and shakily face the day one more time.

Now, in an effort to heal my shattered life, I'm slowly learning to redefine my sense of self, my identity in this strange and scary new world without her, to think in terms of 'I' instead of 'We', while at the same time keep her memory alive in my heart.

I will make it, I will survive, I will somehow learn to be whole again but in a different way than before, and when the tough days come back again, I will always have today, the comforting memory of this 'Good Day' to fall back on.

Waking up from my reveries, I focus back on Max, my only daily companion these days, as he too, healing from his loss, enjoys the day. His inquisitive nose intrigued by the pungent odor of last fall's decaying leaves, he decides to investigate further and scratches the ground with an awkward paw to uncover the newly grown fresh tender grass shoots, a welcomed sign of the summer to come...the never-ending circle of life.

Today is made of my yesterdays, and tomorrow is made of my today.

As I bask in the little success of my article, I cherish my short episodes of freedom and try to make the best of them. I so hope that they would come more often, but unfortunately, they do not and, after a short reprieve, the dark cresting wave falls again and I soon find myself back into the depth of despair and sadness.

Suicidal thoughts

I've always wondered why people give up on life and kill themselves. It was always a mystery to me that a struggling person could not find enough courage and strength to face his/her hardships with pride and dignity. I sadly have to admit that often in my life I looked upon these people with disdain and contempt and compared them to wet noodles and lazy whining slouches. My life has not always been a picnic either, but through it all, in the end I always stood tall. I was bullied and beaten up at school but I fought back. At a very young age I was abused by a homosexual uncle but eventually I fought back and grew out of it. When I lost a job I found another one, and when I suffered the devastating traumatic loss of my young son, after crying endlessly for days, I picked myself up and went on with my life. Herein, courage triumphed over grief.

Because I always thought of myself as a strong-willed individual capable of facing the worst hardships, I had the tendency to be intolerant of people who were not at my level on this and considered them weak and unreliable. But on a very special day all this changed dramatically and I never perceived life the same way again.

One dreary February afternoon, coming back to my stuffy house after an unsatisfactory walk in the park, I had a life-changing experience. The last few days had been horrible and so emotionally charged that any attempts to ease my debilitating stabbing pain were futile. I was desperate and just did not know what to do. I was lost and disoriented like never before. At the end of my roll, I felt I had no strength to talk to anyone, nor did I feel like it. The walls of my little house were dangerously closing in on me, crushing my lungs mercilessly. I could not breathe and kept gasping for air. My weak shaking legs could barely hold me up and my out-of-whack heart was pounding so wildly I thought it could burst through my chest at any moment. I felt more alone than ever. I missed Louise tremendously and everywhere I looked I could not escape the sight of her beautiful face. It suddenly dawned on me then that the only place I could be, the only place I wanted to be, was with her. The severity of my pain and desperation was so overwhelming that at one point my legs gave out on me and I lay down crouching on the floor miserably, in gut-wrenching agony.

Completely broken and subdued, in a desperate attempt to breathe I momentarily raised my head upwards and for some unknown reason opened my teary eyes briefly and stared at the open kitchen cupboard. There it was, my way out, the answer to my precarious predicament: freedom! It was right there in front of me: two 250 ml bottles of liquid morphine and 24 patches of topical morphine, enough to kill a horse. The liquid would put me out quickly and the patches would finish me off slowly. The stash had been left there by the nursing staff after Louise died. It was begging to be abused.

I was in some kind of a trance and my thoughts were traveling at a hundred miles an hour deliberating on my next move. Man, it would be so easy; plaster myself with the deadly morphine patches, gulp the sweet liquid and *Voilà!* I'm off to see the wizard and disappear from this crazy world, no more pain, no more agony. I'd be gone and with Louise forever. So tempting, so enticing, I was in such despair that at this point, the thought of dying was a blessing. The horror of committing such a despicable act wasn't even a consideration. I was in the grips of the indescribable burning pains of hell and I needed relief immediately. Something was holding me back though. Some kind of energy was pulling me the other way, and like in an emotional tug-of-war, I was torn between the beast and the angel fighting inside of me. It was literally a struggle for life or death, and, in the end, those few minutes of hesitation allowed me the time necessary to realize the foolishness of what I was about to do.

After having been in the grips of despair, helplessness and agony, I can now understand better why some desperate soul would go all the way through and take their own life, and how no one is sheltered from this weakness. In the end what counts, though, is that I didn't do it and walked away, an act that separates the strong from the weak, the choice I made.

Edgar Cayce, one of the greatest prophets in modern times, proclaims that a person under great duress and with an intellect completely broken down may experience a period of grace, be touched by a Divine spark and be blessed with strength, inspiration and courage. I draw a parallel between Cayce's period of grace and Zen Buddhism's brief glimmer of enlightenment which also elevates the mind to higher spheres of understanding. Zen claims that one can achieve illumination by killing the 'ego,' either by extreme meditation or by trying to solve koans. Koans are complicated riddles impossible to understand by intellectual processing only. The goal is to force the practitioner to exhaust its thinking abilities, break down its conscious barriers and allow enlightenment to set in.

I don't know what happened to me that day, but I suspect that some kind of mysterious force intervened in my favor to help steer my life towards a different course and not end my life. Was it a Divine period of grace, a brief spark of enlightenment, inspiration from a spirit guide, Louise sending me a message from the other side to hang on, or simply that out of deep despair, I let go and succeeded in tapping into my inner self and drew from my own strength? I guess I'll never know for sure and I will always remember that moment in time as a major mystical turning point in my life. God, Buddha, gurus, mystics and parapsychologists of all kinds, from now on I will keep a positive doubt about the veracity of your claims on the unknown. My life-changing experience expanded my consciousness further and I am grateful for it.

The roller-coaster ride of good days/bad days goes on and on still and if I am to survive this I need to get a serious grip on myself and do what needs to be done; I can't live like this forever. I need to structure a plan of action, gather up my strengths and strategize. Breathing exercises are the first to come to mind as they have always been my safety net through adversity. Although I have been practicing 'Pranayama' (yogic breathing techniques) for many years, this time would be the most serious effort I would ever give it. I don't seem to have a choice; pain is the absolute motivator and I am overwhelmed by it.

As I am planning my strategy, I remember how breathing exercises literally saved my life when my young son was killed 27 years ago. If it wouldn't have been for 'Kapalabhati,' my favorite cleansing breathing technique, I don't know how it would have all ended. I was so devastated and shocked that I couldn't even eat a single morsel of food for a whole week. At the funeral, I looked like a zombie and almost fainted in church. For weeks after, I was useless and depressed and so full of pain that listening to music or playing my piano was impossible as these gestures only increased my sorrows. I truly believe that, along with my sheer will to survive, the practice of Pranayama was instrumental in my recovery. Now for the second major loss of my life I will try to rely on its magic again. I hope and pray that I can make it work once more, for I am desperate and I sense that it is my last resort.

I will also include another psychological deprogramming technique: progressive desensitization or disconnecting strategies (decathecting). Both are similar methods whereby a person learns to detach oneself progressively from the pain associated with a life event or the loss of a person.

In my practice as a therapeutic counselor, I had successfully developed a deprogramming method that incorporated both techniques. I will start my self-therapy with that. Also, I will increase the length and intensity of my Tai Chi practices and my Zen meditations. Up to now, I have only made lame and superficial attempts at their practice and thus did not reap many noticeable benefits. But I can change that, now that I am able to grasp at those momentary sparks of energy brought about by my brief instants of clarity. "I can and I will make this work," I affirm to myself.

The best time of the day will be mid-afternoon, I decide. For the longest time, this period of the day has always been a dead zone for me, and since my loss it is even worst. Although the emptiness that Louise left when she passed away fills every minute of my days, it is the period between four and six o'clock in the afternoon that is the worst. I don't know what it is, some kind of hollowness in the atmosphere that magically appears to have amplified tenfold since I'm alone in the house. It seems like the perfect time.

February 12, 2011

My first session

It's 4:30 in the afternoon and I've just come back from walking along the river and shopping in town. I'm feeling OK I guess, in a kind of neutral mental state. But the minute I enter the house an awful feeling of emptiness begins to take life again and I am instantly dragged down by the heavy chains of grief. Remembering my determination to do everything possible to snap out of this, I drop my bags on the kitchen counter, take my coat off and rapidly climb up the stairs to the second floor and proceed straight to my new room: just a little useless empty nook facing my bedroom door; I had turned it into a cute and comfy meditation sanctuary, complete with meditation futon and bench. I do not believe that all this paraphernalia is necessary to meditate properly, but I wanted to create an atmosphere, to make it fun and inviting.

I kneel on the futon in the traditional *zazen* position, sitting on a bench that bridges over my calves and under my butt, rest my hands on my thighs with palms facing up, and close my eyes. I easily focus on the stabbing pain in the middle of my stomach as I allow the image of Louise to fill my mental space and I begin my cleansing breath exercise. Kapalabhati is a breathing exercise that consists of a series of forced and sudden expulsions of air. I have used that exercise in a technique I developed especially to help clients alleviate the overflow of negative energy bottled up in their solar plexus. So, when I am totally absorbed in the moment, I suddenly and forcefully contract my abdominal muscles to force the air out of my lungs. At the same time and with each expulsion, I also concentrate on letting go of the pain associated with Louise's image. I repeat the process over and over again until her mental image does not trigger pain anymore. The momentary reprieve I experience now will not last long, of that I am certain, but eventually, with time and repetition, the negative emotional connection will dissipate permanently. My soul, thus free of the unhealthy attachment, will eventually allow me to smile when I think of her.

I stop and rest for a few minutes while I let the cleansing process complete itself. It always takes a short period of time before one feels its liberating effects entirely. When this is achieved, I begin my second breathing exercise which aims at recharging and boosting my nervous system and is the ideal complement to Kapalabhati. It is a martial arts breathing method aimed at increasing my 'chi' or 'ki' (vital energy) in the second chakra (one of the energy centers in the human body), just 2 inches below the navel. This particular chakra is believed by the martial arts masters to be the center of gravity of the body and responsible for accomplishing great feats of strength when one is properly trained to manipulate its awesome power.

In preparation for the chi-building exercise, I reposition myself in the zazen position, let my hands sit on my lap and form a circle with my thumb and index finger. With eyes closed, I then inhale a certain amount of air that I immediately let go again slowly through a controlled exhalation; I gently exhale and push the air out until my lungs are completely empty. At this stage, I breathe in slowly while imagining that the flow of inhaled oxygen travels through my lungs and settles in my lower belly, swelling it like a balloon. Then, holding my breath to trap the air in that balloon, I again contract my abdominal girth and, while holding the contraction, I count slowly up to 30. Then, at that point, I abruptly relax my stomach muscles, exhale suddenly and relax.

After about ten minutes of that, it is now time to begin my Zen meditation. To create a bit of atmosphere (not necessary, mind you, but it helps me get into the mood), I light up a stick of sandalwood incense and launch my CD player. As the soft sound of the *shakuhachi* Japanese flute enchants the air, I half close my eyes and start staring blankly at the floor 3 feet ahead of me. The constant flow of air going in and out of my lungs is regulated by the rhythm of my counting; inhale—one, exhale—two, inhale—one, exhale—two, and so on and so forth until I reach a series of ten inhalations/exhalations and then I start again. If a thought comes to mind, I do not pay attention to it but refocus my attention on counting my breath. Eventually, after 30 to 60 minutes of this, I enter a light state of heightened consciousness where according to the books I read I should become 'one with the universe' and free myself momentarily from the bounds of the physical world.

Sounds great in theory, but the actual fact is that it takes years of strict discipline to even come close to reaching a higher state of consciousness, let alone enlightenment. Although being illuminated is not my goal at this stage, I am nevertheless a bit discouraged by my poor performances: my sessions are tarred with an incredibly undisciplined mind, I have great difficulty keeping my thoughts from wandering and I can't remain focused on my breathing for more than a couple of minutes at a time. At the realization of this, my aspirations to become a Zen master, if that was ever an issue, evaporate totally the minute I try to unfold my poor aching body from my precarious position: my butt cheeks hurt and my legs are so numbed that I have to fall forward, flat on my face, and remain there until the blood flows into my legs again and I can stand up. Pitiful.

It's a start though and I will not let little details like not being able to walk straight for ten minutes after each session deter me from my goal. *I will do this*, I think. *No matter what, I will do it.*

Encouraged by my newfound determination, I walk back

down to my kitchen and prepare to do my Tai Chi session. I have altered the original technique so that the exercise can be performed in a confined space, such as a small hotel room or a kitchen as in my case. Tai Chi, which is often referred to as 'the walking meditation,' is ideal to help keep my mind off of things while allowing me to recondition my over-stressed body. Mastering Tai Chi takes years of training, and even though I am just a novice, executing the complicated movements forces me to focus my attention long enough to help keep my rut at bay. But there is more to the Chinese marvel, much more. Aside from the obvious physical benefits, Tai Chi's wonder is that it has a powerful effect on the body/mind's energy levels. It promotes proper circulation of vital energy and stimulates the lymphatic system, thus increasing the body's potential for self-healing.

Thirty minutes of practice completes my routine for the day and I feel somewhat better with myself. Well, at least for now, and I refuse to even think of how long this good feeling will last until the darkness returns. I have so much more to do, so much further to go, it's almost discouraging to think about it. But for now I turn the page and, hanging on by a thread, I concentrate on the moment, brushing away all thought and expectations of possible incoming storms.

Chapter 6

Pre-Loss:
April 1, 2008

A time of denial, confusion and disorganization
Shock, resentment, depression and acceptance

First chemotherapy

The ride to Ottawa was nice and smooth and the weatherman's predictions were correct, for once: sunny and no threat of snow that day. *Great,* I thought. *It's looking good for the trip back home too.* Even though the road was dry and safe, I felt shaky and wary. Louise was silent and stared straight ahead with a look of concern that said it all.

Numbed at the expectation of what was to come, we barely talked for the hour it took us to arrive at the hospital. Our destination, the eighth floor of the Ottawa General Hospital, is where the ovarian cancer treatment department was located, and we were not all that keen to get there. We did arrive eventually though, and after parking the car we entered directly into the cancer center and walked nervously on to the elevators.

The elevator bell sounded its usual ding and the door opened up, giving way to a series of long corridors filled with stretchers, linen carts, disembodied voices talking over intercoms, and the usual hospital apparatuses. Reluctantly walking out of the elevator, we headed off towards the nurses' station neighboring the dreaded room. Ah! That mysterious room, I remember it well now as I passed it so many times in my previous visits to the hospital during Louise's stay after the surgery. Every time I walked in front of it, I felt it projected a kind of mystifying aura that somehow made me weak in the knees. It freaked me out, to be more precise, but at the same time, it also triggered an extreme sense of curiosity that I could not ignore. *What is going on in this last resort for the hopeful walking dead?* I asked myself every time I dared to give the room a furtive look. I could only imagine the worst, and over and over again, the scary scene of people lying down on beds, helplessly wired up to convoluted plastic tubes, getting their veins pumped up full of burning chemicals, came to mind. How awful it must feel for them to patiently sit for hours in this torture room, desperately hanging on to their last stretch of life, hoping for a miracle! The mere idea of the whole scenario was intolerable, and with hurried steps I would walk away from the place thinking, *Not for now*, an empty brush-off if I ever made one, as I knew darn well that 'now' would come too soon.

Back from my little mental escapade, I came to grips with the hard fact that Louise was there now, in this time and space, waiting her turn to get fueled up with the toxic poison. What's this going to do to her system? I mean face it, this stuff is so strong and toxic that we were told to wear gloves to clean the toilet bowl for the first two times Louise urinated after the treatment. I was also seriously warned to use extreme care if I dared to relieve myself right after Louise used the toilet, otherwise I could 'fry' my little 'man things' if they hung down too close to the contaminated saucer. What a horrible thought, eew, who wants that?

I couldn't believe we were there; it didn't seem possible that this was happening to us, to me: chemotherapy, the big 'C.' Oh my gawd this was so scary and unreal. I wanted to run out of there as if the plague was after me, but Louise without flinching an inch waltzed right in there, lay down on an empty bed and waited coolly for the attending nurse. If she was nervous, she hid it very well. Wasn't she scared and depressed like me? Wasn't she resentful that even though she always worked hard at taking care of herself, she still ended up in this horrendous place? If I were her, I would be beside myself with fear and I don't know how dignified I could remain. *Ah! My trooper, I am so very proud of you*, I thought at that moment.

"Hi, my name is Angie and I will be looking after you today," we suddenly heard from an approaching nurse. She was a friendly-looking middle-aged, full-bodied grey-haired woman who spoke with a soft and gentle voice. According to her demeanor and assuredness, she looked like she'd been doing this job for a long time. *Reassuring*, I thought. After briefing Louise on what was to come, and requesting that she fill out a bunch of forms, Angie hooked Louise up to a monitor and proceeded with the customary pre-treatment tests: blood pressure, pulse, temperature, etc. She also consulted Louise's charts containing the previous day's blood-test results to verify if she was up to taking the treatment. When Angie decided that everything was cool, she expertly and gently stuck a needle in Louise's arm and connected it to a tube hooked up to a clear plastic bag hanging over Louise's head from the bed pole. The treatment was to last approximately five to six hours. I sat comfortably in the lounge chair by the bed, picked up one of the many magazines lying around and prepared for the long day ahead.

Reading did not come easily though, and my worried mind was unsettled and wandered off continuously. As I kept a monitoring eye on Louise, I gave in to my reveries and slowly allowed my mind to slip back in time, reminiscing on the past few horrendous months.

Wednesday, March 15, 2008
Removing the stitches

It was seven at night and Louise and I were cooling our butts in the doctor's office waiting to have her stitches from her hysterectomy removed and we were prepared for the long wait to come. You see, our GP offered this after-hour service without appointments (which we appreciated, mind you), but the bummer was that we had to arrive two hours before the last scheduled appointment was over at 9 p.m. It's all very nice of him to do this, but one has to consider that the only reason we accepted this opportunity is because the first scheduled appointment available with him was in three months' time. Yes, you read correctly, our very own family doctor could not schedule us in before three months' time. Pity! Where have the good old days gone when we could see our doctor at a day's notice? But I shouldn't complain as the alternative would have been to drive three hours back and forth to the hospital to have the procedure done and still probably wait for another couple of hours in the sitting room. So I guess we ended up winning on this one, but still!

Normally the long wait would not have been such a problem, but Louise was in a considerable degree of discomfort and was very weak and restless. I also had concerns about the redness along the scar on her tummy and that the stitches might be painful to take off. Yes, yes, I know, I'm a worrywart, but I can't help it. My darn protective instinct always seems to want to take over in moments like this; what can I say, I am what I am, right?

Anyhow, my fears were unfounded and the visit went well: the redness around the wound was normal, and aside from one nasty reluctant stitch near the navel, everything was cool. As we walked out of the doctor's office, the good news we had just received caused me to reflect for a short moment on the body's miraculous abilities to recover from tragedy. Yes, indeed, and 'tragic' was the only word I could use to describe the horrendous two weeks that Louise went through following her surgery.

March 1, 2008
I feel helpless as Louise is horribly sick

I remember how powerless and inadequate I felt at that time for not being able to do more to help alleviate her sufferings. I somehow felt guilty and frustrated for not possessing some kind of powers that could magically make all of this go away. I was devastated and overwhelmed with grief as I witnessed her withering away in an out-of-control downward spiral as she was struck by a massive and devastating gastro-enteritis. I had never in my life seen anyone be so sick. My heart is heavy and my gut hurts as I flash back to that moment. She was overwhelmed by dozens of uncontrollable episodes of violent vomiting and horrible spouts of diarrhea per day. At times the spasms were so strong and violent that her hands, arms and feet would paralyze mercilessly (tetanize). Then, trying to remain calm as best as I could, with a shaky voice, I would have to guide her into relaxation to help alleviate her terrible anxiety and calm down the involuntary muscle contractions in her extremities.

But the most atrocious part in all of this was that every time she was sick, the fresh stitches holding her tummy together threatened to rip out, tearing her skin brutally and leaving a nasty open gash. A horrible thought! I had to hold and press a pillow to her stomach each time she threw up, in an effort to minimize the possible damage done by the vomiting motion. Aside from these humble interventions, the extent of my implication in the whole heartbreaking scene was limited to sponging, bathing, feeding, running errands and bringing her emotional support, that's it. Quite destabilizing for me to feel so useless in front of such a drama, but little did I know then that the worst was yet to come.

The mere thought of seeing her like this drove me absolutely crazy, but I could only stand there, like a helpless idiot, feeling guilty for not being able to do more for her. It was a hurtful, pitiful and horrendous sight and I was resentful at the world for allowing this to happen. *How much can a person take for heaven's sake, leave her alone, hasn't she had enough?* I thought angrily and ready to pick a fight with the 'Big Guy.' But God's wicked and twisted sense of humor did not let up for another seven dreadful days and she must have lost at least 18 pounds during that trying time. She was so exhausted and weak that she could not walk without support for the little distance from the bathroom to the living room where she constantly lay on the couch, totally wasted. I would massage her overstrained back and recoil with sympathy every time she yelped out in pain. In all of the times I felt helpless during her voyage, this period must have been the worst, and many times I prayed I could miraculously assume some of her pain so she could have a rest for a while. But unfortunately nature would not have it. It would not respond to my pleading and bargaining. Life sucks sometimes. It does not care; it just is.

Louise got better eventually and I managed somehow to regain my bearings. I was very emotional after that episode and I felt an urgent need to vent and to express how proud I was of Louise's courageous behavior through all of this. After that dramatic episode, my heart was raw, confused and in an out-of-control emotional turmoil and I could not even come close to being able to express myself coherently. Words would just not come out properly; the undercurrent of repressed emotions was just too strong. So in view of all of this, I decided to put pen to paper and write her a letter; I thought it would be easier and more efficient to talk to her this way.

Hi Honey!

You must really wonder why I'm writing this letter to you, but bear with me, it will be self-explanatory later on.

Ever since we received the dreadful news about your health, my life has turned into a veritable emotional whirlwind and I can only assume how nightmarish it must have been for you too.

Through all the difficult episodes that you've gone through since then, you exhibited the strength and courage I always thought you had and I am very proud of you for that. It is on the dreadful surgery day though that my esteem for you turned into awe. I can still picture you holding your head up high while stumbling on wobbly legs as you valiantly made your way towards the pre-op room. Your allure then was that of a Grand Lady walking bravely to an uncertain fate and I could never have been more impressed by that. Know that this image will forever remain imprinted in my mind.

I could have spoken these words to you eventually, but I prefer to set them on paper instead for your keeping; 'words spoken fly away, words written stay.' Life throws curves at us all the time, and should adversity ever strike you again, remember how great you were once and how great you can be again.

Honey, you are an extraordinary woman and I love you with all my heart.

Always,

Me

Back at the hospital, I was taken out of my reverie by the oncology nurse coming into the room to finalize the procedure: "Congratulations, Mrs Milot, you just completed your first treatment and it went very well," she said. I would agree with that comment if it weren't for the fact that the medical team had to interrupt the session in order to administer Louise a sedative in an effort to stop the scary heart palpitations she was having. Panic attack, they said, and it is common in new chemotherapy patients apparently. But as I would learn later, chemotherapy could also occasionally cause a nasty heart attack, an important little fact that was hidden from us. Would we have wanted to know though? Maybe not, maybe it was best this way and it would probably have added to Louise's already high stress level, who knows. But it makes me feel good to bitch a little; it's liberating.

Finally, five hours later, the ordeal is over and I can take Louise back home, but not before she swallows a little yellow pill. A second one is also given to her and she must make sure to take it the next day, otherwise she could be violently sick with nausea. "No problem," I said with determination, "I'll make sure she takes it." The mere thought of vomiting sends me into a frenzied panic and I was surely not going to let Louise suffer more and spill her guts out in front of me again, not if I could help it. It was now time to start implementing our back-up plan: an alternative natural treatment meant to alleviate the side effects of chemotherapy while increasing its efficiency. Will it work? Only time will tell.

Chapter 7

Post-Loss:
March 2011

The dangers of unresolved grief: anger, resentment and rage
Relinquishing old attachments
Readjusting and adapting to the new life
Creating a new relationship with the deceased
Creating a new identity and new ways to function in the new world
Reinvesting energy formally absorbed by the old attachments into other activities and causes
Reinforcing coping mechanisms

The gym was not very busy today; very quiet and, aside from a few overzealous bodybuilders furiously pumping iron while exhibiting a sparkling set of bright white teeth in an uninviting grimace that says, *Go away and don't bother me*, there is nothing much else to see. Not even a good-looking girl in sight as I would have expected. Zilch. Boring!

Let's crawl back home slowly and hope I don't get honked at too often by hurried drivers following me and pissed off at being slowed down by my 'I don't give a crap' sorry-ass slow driving. Between the 60 minutes it takes me to travel back and forth to the gym and my actual time in there, I manage to kill a miserable two and a half hours of my unending day. Wow, now what? But I shouldn't ask as I know darn well what I need to do once I get back into my mind-numbing abode: tedious disconnecting exercises. Oh joy, what a blast! I always resist that phase of the program and, although efficient, I find it difficult and draining emotionally. The sessions always bring me back into an underlying cesspool of repressed emotions, a world I'd rather forget, but cannot, must not. In fact, facing these feelings is mandatory if

I want to get over this. Making excuses to avoid my mental workout is not an option and I have to stick to my plan, regardless.

Back at home, once again as I open the kitchen door, I'm instantly assaulted by a powerful sense of emptiness and I start choking again. "Damn it," I say out loud in frustration. *I have to do this, I don't have a choice,* and hurriedly start making my way up the stairs to my meditation corner.

April 2011

Ditching Louise's car

I have been doing my exercises for a while now and I seem to have made some small progress. Before, when I did the cleansing breath, I could only visualize a mental image of Louise, but now I have graduated to looking at an actual picture of her. My plan is to place her photo at the farthest distance possible in the room and stare at it while performing my breathing exercises. I will repeat the process over and over again, each time bringing the picture a little closer to me until the suffering associated with the memory of her loss dissipates. Psychologists call this method 'progressive desensitization' and it is extremely efficient.

To grieve properly, I need to create a new relationship with Louise while keeping her memory alive in my heart. I need to create a new identity for myself and develop new ways to function in the post-loss world. As difficult as it may be, disconnecting from the suffering associated with the memory of the lost happy couple that we once were is what I unwillingly need to do. I must now think in terms of 'I' instead of 'we' if I want to survive in my new world, my new reality. Losing Louise who lovingly shared my life for 38 years is like losing half of me. Now I need to become a wizard and invent some kind of magical trick to patch myself up and become whole again. At least, this is how it feels, and at times I seriously doubt my abilities to do so. I concede the show must go on and I relentlessly start over a new set of breathing exercises.

The days become weeks and I am making more and more progress with my exercises. There are the usual ups and downs of course and the downs of my wild roller-coaster ride seem to be less dramatic nowadays. Time though remains a problem, as I have too much of it. After spending 24 hours a day, seven days a week for three years taking care of Louise while she was sick, the space that she left when she died is immeasurable and has become an extremely heavy burden on me. Minutes seem like hours and hours feel like days and I am fighting like a lion to reorganize my distorted concept of time. It is hard, very hard, not to think of her and to ignore the sick feeling of loss haunting me, when everything I see, smell and touch sorrowfully reminds me of our time together, who we were and who we are not anymore.

At regular intervals in my quest to rise from the ashes of loss, I have felt the need to let go and dispose of material things that triggered too much pain and kept me attached to my pre-loss era. Louise's belongings, her clothes, the memorabilia, and most of the personal and business files that we had in common have all gone, and if I have not outright gotten rid of them, I have already learned to disconnect emotionally from those objects. The pictures though I have not touched yet; that will come later, much later. Some say that they should be packed away in a box and not looked at before we feel we are ready for them. That sometimes can take years for obvious reasons, and I sure as hell am not ready for that yet.

Part of my regular routine is to go out after dinner and take a long relaxing walk by the St Lawrence River bordering Cornwall's Lamoureux Park. I always find it soothing to lazily walk on the cute winding pathways filled with sumptuous black willow trees overhanging the water like giant bonsais. I love watching people enjoying the picturesque sight of adorable colorful ducks carelessly treading water in search of a few bread crumbs thrown to them illegally by laughing children. But, as so often happens with grief, the whole scene is suddenly overshadowed by a painful wave of sadness as my attention is drawn to an adorable couple walking by, lovingly holding hands. For a short fleeting moment the sting of loss reappears and I feel more alone than ever.

These unfortunate occurrences have become habitual though and I must not let them deter me from my daily routine. Life does not care about my misery, the world will go on turning with or without me, and I must learn to deal with that in my pursuit of rebirth.

So, after washing the dishes like a good boy, I rush out the door, jump into my car and take off for my much-needed refuge by the water. My car...hum, actually it was Louise's car and that's a story in itself. I will need to take care of that situation, and soon.

Brand new, she had bought it some time ago on a whim. It is cute, white and comfortable. It has a tan leather interior and is fully equipped. I guess that she would not have purchased it if she would have known of her medical condition, but hey, who knows the future, right? Anyway, as comfortable as it was for her, it has always been a bit awkward for my long skinny legs as it restricts movements when I am at the wheel. Mentally bitching every time I bang my right knee on the center console, I keep worrying about how badly this leg could be injured if I were to get involved in a car accident. That fact weighed heavily in my consideration to change the car, but was not my main reason.

You see, the more I drive that darn car, the more it grows on me, and not in a good way. The minute I sit behind the wheel I feel as if some mysterious force wants to take over and drive off for Ottawa. So many long sad trips to the hospital have been done in that vehicle that it seems like it's possessed and has finally developed a mind of its own. Fear, pain and anxiety are imprinted in every fiber of the driver's compartment and I can sense them each time I enter the vehicle. It makes me sick and brings me back into a place where I do not want to be. It did not use to be like that in the first months after Louise died, but now this situation has become insufferable and I must do something about it. Time to act and I'm off to the car dealership...

There it is; it stands out like an apparition among the hundreds of other vehicles parked in the dealer's lot waiting for new parents. It's grey with a black leather interior and it looks very sleek and powerful, at least the areas that are still showing under the pile of snow covering it. I'm thunderstruck and I fall in love with it immediately, even before trying it out, even without sitting in it, even without hearing the entrancing soft roaring sound of its mufflers. It's a Cadillac CTS and I want it. Needless to say, I am not a hard sell and Janice, the car sales person, never had it so easy. After a quick test drive, sales arrangements are made and like a proud daddy I drive my 'baby' back home. I always loved that car, but Louise would have nothing to do with it. "It looks square, boxy, aggressive (I definitely did not agree with that) and I don't like it," she bluntly stated. So of course, like a good chap willing to keep harmony in the family, I restrained from getting one and suffered, so to speak, in silence for many years. Nobody can stop me now though. I have no one to please but myself; the perks of living alone...well, maybe one of the few rare ones.

Buying that car was to me quite a revelation. First and foremost, of course, is the fact that I am not at the mercy of a haunted vehicle anymore. Secondly, my Caddie is a real jewel and is everything I expected it to be: luxurious, great-looking and comfortable; no more knocking my right knee on the center console, thank you and *merci beaucoup* as we say in French. This car is built for tall long-legged Cadillac enthusiasts like me. Sitting my butt in the soft-leathered heated driver seat is quite a thrill and I enjoy every minute of it; the multi-position adjustable seat fits my body perfectly and I feel as if a pair of comforting arms hugs me lovingly.

Thirdly, I have to admit that what draws me the most to that addictive machine are the buzzwords floating around about its performances: a driver's car, hugs to the road, handles tight turns marvelously, high-speed maneuverability. "It's when you push it hard that it shows its true colors," the experts say. "The more you ask, the more it gives." "It loves to be driven."

The mature part of me does not want to put these statements to the test of course, but my wild side is almost salivating at the mere thought of it. I sadly fear that the main reason why I'm attracted so much to my newfound buddy is that it seems to bring out the beast in me; some kind of adolescent bravado behavior that is reawakened through sporadic bouts of unresolved grief having to do with hidden anger and resentment. *Will this have the best of me?* I ask myself. I have a feeling I'm about to find out.

The nasty side of unresolved grief

It's six o'clock at night and I'm at home, sunk in my comfy leather couch, sipping my second Scotch, my hands cold and trembling (not from the alcohol, I can assure you!). I'm shaking my head in bewilderment at what had just happened a couple of hours ago. Boy, what a day this has been. Never in my life would I have dared driving so recklessly, an unconscious death-wish?

Unresolved grief is a bizarre phenomenon and this aspect of grief is maybe the sneakiest and most untimely, if not to say the most dangerous of all as we will see. Unexpectedness is probably what I find the most difficult when it comes to dealing with grief; the way it manages to creep up on me at the most inconvenient of times. As Allen Funt from the old *Candid Camera* television show used to say, "Anytime, anywhere, we'll catch you when you're least expecting it," and today I had the perfect example of this.

Grief comes in waves and only needs a trigger to act out. Today, my trigger was a long and winding deserted country road.

The ride

I'm driving back home after having had a nice lunch with a friend and I'm feeling quite good, if not a little pumped up on caffeine due to the last double espresso I had hurriedly ingested before taking the road. As scheduled, I stop at the Lancaster provincial police station to report damages made to my car by the previous week's wind storm. The station, which is the first one coming into Ontario from Quebec via Highway 401, is surprisingly modern and impressive for a rural station, but when I try to get in, I butt my head on a locked door. Wondering what the heck is going on, I finally get wise and decide to read the notice stuck on the door: 'Closed for vacation.' Bewildered, I smile to myself thinking, *Only in the country, man, only in the country.* At that instant, I find myself transported into an old episode of the famous Andy Griffith's *Mayberry* television series where a similar handwritten poster wedged on the police station door said: 'Closed for the day, gone fishing.' Who the heck has ever heard of a police station left unattended? But as I will find out later, only the adminis-trative office employees are cooling off their heels, not the local gendarmes.

Discombobulated, I walk back to my car and proceed to make the trip back home. As I am pulling out of the parking lot though, something strange occurs in me and I 'snap' as I stare at the enticing road ahead. At that particular moment, my sense of reality is distorted. I feel beside myself and I am not seeing just a road, I am staring at a stretch of asphalt begging to be desecrated and violated. It's as if my wild side is taking over, and in an almost uncontrollable youthful boldness, right in front of the police station, I load an aggressive jazz CD on my stereo, max out the volume, slip on an imaginary pair of tight leather driving gloves, look ahead and say out loud with a daring voice: "OK, ROAD, let's see what you've got!" and I step on it, leaving a trail of burnt rubber behind me. Man, what a rush!

The feelings I experience as I get lost in that moment are

nothing less than exhilarating. Each gas pedal kick-down I make dramatically increases the speed of my vehicle and transforms the exciting groovy roar of my baby's muffler along with the entrancing racing sound of its intricate engine into an unparalleled experience. My blood boils in my veins and I'm like a teen having forbidden sex for the first time. I feel awesome, a weird mixture of guilt, fear, exhilaration, joy and excitement all at the same time. I know that what I am doing is wrong, but like a possessed man caught up in the thrill of the forbidden, I do it anyway. I'm aware of a growing sense of freedom and trepidation like I've never experienced before. The more I step on the gas pedal, the more I want to push it as I unwillingly transform myself into some kind of angry devil taking over the car's commands. My speed is way over the safe limit but I don't even want to look at the speedometer anymore. Negotiating the steep curves of the narrow winding road at alarming speed gives me a kick that is almost orgasmic and brings me to marvel on the fact that the Caddie sticks to the road like a champ; not even a single screech from the over-stressed tires. "Man, what a car," I marvel.

My wild and entrancing ride goes on for a while and I'm so lost in the thrill of the moment that I do not even notice the first signs of civilization and ignore the usual speed-limit notification as I enter the village where I live. As one can expect, the disturbing manifestations of my crazy behavior do not remain unnoticed by 'you know who' and the inevitable happens. My ass is fried and 'Inspector Clouseau' appears out of nowhere with blazing flashers and terrifying siren bringing me back to reality. As I'm finally forced to slow down, with heart still racing I pull in front of the village's post office and stare in my back mirror at the incoming trouble. Mr Gendarme steps out of his vehicle wearing a nasty grin. At that moment a disturbing thought pops up in my mind: *Shucks. I'm done!*

As he slowly walks over to my car, I hurriedly struggle to pull myself together and try to look as innocent and naive as I can in an attempt to soften the blow. "What's wrong, officer? Was I speeding?" I stupidly ask after lowering my window to talk to him. "Speeding?" he says with a tone of voice that says it all. "You must be kidding me...I clocked you at 65 miles an hour...the speed limit in the village is 30 miles an hour," he carries on, leaving me no room for explanations. I guess there are none, I must admit. I'm guilty as hell and I know it. I then deduce, though, that I still must have slowed down a bit somehow at one point, because I was riding way faster than that in those back roads. *But let's not tell him that, I've got a feeling that it wouldn't work in my favor*, I think. After he says his piece, he politely asks for my papers and goes back to his car to do whatever policemen do in cases like this.

So as he sits in his black bomber doing his thing, I hesitantly get out of my Caddie, waving to him in a gesture that says, 'I'm crossing over to the post office to get my mail.' He casually waves back at me with an OK sign through his cruiser's windshield. *Hum, strange*, I think, *I usually would be confined to my car while he's verifying if I'm not an escaped prisoner or a wanted terrorist on a mission. Oh well, cool*, I think and proceed across the street to pick up my mail. It's only after coming back from the store that the whole thing starts to get a little bizarre.

Just as I open my car door, I hear a voice calling my name (my first name, that is). *Weird*, I think. Usually in past similar situations, cops exhibited a polite intimidating air and a 'tight ass attitude' as they called me 'Sir.' But no, not this guy, and in a reassuring but intriguing manner he addresses me like so: "Pierre, would you come over here please?" *Whoa, what's going on here?* I think suspiciously and, intrigued as to what kind of tactic he's pulling on me, I walk cautiously towards him. "Ordinarily, I would never do this," he says, "but would you please take a look at the radar screen through the window of my cruiser and read the speed I clocked you at?" as he points with his finger at a gizmo inside the car. It was not a question, but a clear directive.

Ouch! 65 mph flashing in bright red; no denying that at this point and instantly visions of dollar bills with wings pouring out of my wallet start to float around. Vague images of prison bars and handcuffs are not far behind.

Getting even more bizarre now, and to what phenomenon I can attribute what is about to happen, I can only guess. The young officer must be psychic, or maybe he reads a big sign flashing over my fat airhead saying, 'Crazy, newly widowed, please handle with care.' I don't know.

But in any event, the young man hands me back my papers and with a nice smile says: "I'll let you off with a warning for now. I don't like to ticket the locals, so please be careful next time."

"Geez…Aaah…hum…well, thanks, officer," I awkwardly spit out and, completely stunned, I walk back to my car. I can't say that I feel relieved or appreciative though, for at this time I am still under the influence of my crazy rush, and strangely enough the thought of losing demerit points and paying a huge fine isn't truly a concern; actually I really couldn't care less. It's only after a few hours of winding down at home that I realize what I have done, and I almost have a fit.

I can barely face the fact that I behaved in such an irresponsible manner. I'm usually Mr Cool, the guy who leisurely strolls along at turtle speed while listening to smooth jazz and occasionally pulling onto the side of the road to let other hurried drivers pass by. What just went on here? Dazzled and confused, after much deliberation I come to the inescapable conclusion that grief is involved, unresolved grief, to be more precise. Reflecting back, I realize that in the past three years when Louise was under cancer treatment, our lives were so very restricted that we almost never left home. She was always too weak to travel, and in the off chance that we did try a furtive escape, it was always cut short by a pressing retreat back at the house. The only time we did force the outing was to go out for her treatments at the hospital.

No fun there, only stress, and lots of it! Being her sole caretaker was a 24-hours-a-day job, and as the years went by it progressively turned into a way of life for me. I grew into the grips of restrictions so progressively that it became a normalcy for me. I did not think twice about it and I did what I had to do, no afterthoughts, no regrets, no resentment, and I probably would have done it for the rest of my life if she would not have passed away.

My unexpected little escapade, though, makes me realize that through these three long years I continuously refrained from expressing myself emotionally. Being Louise's sole caretaker meant standing guard 24/7 without flinching. Her physical and emotional needs were so pressing at times that I had to put my own on the back burner; no time to be sick, tired, sad or depressed, no breakdown possible here. That could come later, if it had to come at all, I reasoned. Strength and determination were of the essence and I gave it my best shot.

The fact that I was losing the love of my life, my best friend, my future, my life that could have been but will never be, had to be ignored if I were to survive my ordeal and be an efficient lifesaving buoy for Louise. But I was suffering, I was suffering a lot, and I knew that there would be a price to pay for this later, that these repressed and unresolved emotional grief issues would need to be unleashed at some point, and today was one of those days. On that particular road, in that particular car, at that particular time I snapped and turned into a devil in need of release. That's how dangerous and devastating unresolved grief can be. My temporary release-valve sure enough gave me some kind of solace, but I sense that there are still a few more skeletons hiding in my closet and I need to be careful not to have a repeat performance.

Jokingly I made a promise to myself that while in the process of resolving my grief I would seek a more benign form of expression as a coping strategy. Here's a good idea: why not ride a bicycle to exhaustion, which shouldn't take too long anyway considering the pitiful physical shape I'm in. Oh well, I'll find something eventually, that's what counts.

About the car, I know what you're thinking, and NO, I'm not getting rid of it. Mr Caddie, my good buddy, stays with me, period.

Chapter 8

Pre-Loss:
April 22 to August 2008
Anger, resentment, bitterness, irritability, bargaining

This period was mainly dedicated to completing the five treatments left in the first round of chemotherapy. The rate was one treatment every two to three weeks, and before each session a blood test was required to make sure that Louise's white blood-cell count was high enough to sustain the treatment successfully. The sessions were long, exhausting and scary for her as she always had an aversion for needles to the point that she almost fainted at the mere sight of them. To top it off, her veins were minuscule which made the treatments even more difficult and painful, a fact that was about to transform her life into a real nightmare in the months to come.

Finding a good vein to work with had become quite an undertaking for the oncology nurses. The multitude of tests, blood work, scans and treatments rendered her veins so fragile and sensitive that eventually there was no other choice but to stab her through the veins at the top of her hands. A very sensitive spot and anyone who's ever had an injection there can vouch for that. Imagine spending six to eight hours lying on a bed with a bunch of tubes and needles painfully stuck in your hand while burning liquid is being pumped through your body; it was a soul-troubling experience.

It was terribly hard for me to see her like this, all wired up like a damn robot, wincing and suffering. My protective side was taking quite a beating and at times I wanted to scream my frustrations, rip out all this paraphernalia, take her home, pump her full of painkillers, let nature take its course and allow her to die painlessly in peace and dignity. If only we would have known the outcome of our journey then, this might have spared us a lot of suffering and anguish and would have achieved the same results, but only sooner.

Nevertheless, it was mainly her decision to take the treatments and she would go all the way regardless and I knew it. She was that kind of a person. There was nothing I could do but reluctantly stand guard, 'suck it up' and swallow my resentment.

Little did I know then that shutting my big mouth would also be a prudent attitude to adopt all through these tribulations. As we were soon about to find out, making waves and going outside the 'system' was not a prudent thing to do.

They say it never rains but it pours, and of course, as if the needle stuff was not enough, Louise unbelievably developed an allergic reaction (some sort of horrible reddish and itchy rash at the site of the injection) to the anti-allergic medication. If it wasn't so serious, it'd be laughable; an allergic reaction to an anti-allergy drug. LOL. So of course the injections, which were fast acting, had to be stopped and replaced by a pill to be taken orally. The bummer though is that the pill took longer to kick in, thus making the sessions even longer.

Of course, during the long hours of waiting, I had time to think. Not always a good thing though (for an overactive intellect like mine), and my musing, stemming from fear and resentment, went from cursing all the gods ever known to man to praying and making deals with the same guys. Lying at the bottom of a well of despair, like I was during some of those horrible days, I was willing to reconsider my options. And I did. Just in case I could have been wrong in my views of this crazy world. What if there was a God? What if I was wrong? What if he occasionally listened to poor saps like me? What if I prayed hard enough and made him listen to my plea, convinced him that Louise was a good person worth a blink from him? What if I promised to become a better person dedicated to the service of others, would that help?

But wait, I sarcastically reflected at times, don't miracles occur spontaneously sometimes, like I read in some religious books? I'm waiting, God, do your thing; she's suffering and every minute counts. Don't you have a heart or are you going to feed me the crappy line that you work in mysterious ways...that it's a learning experience for her and for me, that I should have faith and that every good thing happens to him who waits.

I'm watching you, God, you'd better perform; otherwise I'm reverting to believing that you're nothing but an imaginary being and a fabrication created directly out of the twisted minds of somber prophets and greedy kings to suit their purposes. On I went with the pleas and threats, venting my frustrations until I often fell asleep, exhausted and no further ahead than when I started.

Mental note

In retrospect, all through the years that Louise was sick, I must have gone through this bargaining and threatening routine a hundred times, and an elusive god still remained silent and unresponsive, even to my threats. Who knows? Maybe it was her karma to end her life in pain and suffering, something she had to accomplish for the sake of her spiritual growth. I'll never know. *Maybe God does work in mysterious ways for some and not for others,* I wonder. I respect other people's spiritual values and the fact that they may find strength and solace in the belief that a higher being is looking after them, but as for me, I think this is nonsense.

Life is life and it just doesn't care; we are part of nature, and nature is the only true God energy as far as I'm concerned. We're all caught up in the same never-ending cycle of living and dying. Pain is part of the evolutionary process, therefore it is not good or bad; it just is. Karma is karma, and in spite of our greatest efforts to fly away on our own, we're always dragged back into the learning pathway set for us at birth. Free choice only goes so far.

September to December 2008
More denial, hope, anger and resentment
This period was in an upswing, at least in the beginning. The first round of chemotherapy was finished and it was a rest period for Louise. Her hair had started to grow back again, for which she was grateful. Beauty is in the eye of the beholder and I was never shy of telling her how great she still looked even as a baldy. The colorful scarves that she expertly wrapped around her head only added to her natural beauty.

Another detail to be praised also was the fact that all through the treatments she was always nausea-free. Was it the workings of the little yellow pill taken after each chemo treatment or the mountain of natural supplements I had her ingest in an effort to enhance the efficiency of the treatment and minimize its side effects? Who cares, something worked and it was all that mattered.

Since the storm had calmed down somewhat, we started to look for an alternative health practitioner for the continuation of her treatment. We wanted a therapist who would have a solid understanding of both alternative and conventional medicine, a doctor licensed in both disciplines. Our goal was not only to use natural medicine as an adjunct, but as Louise's main cancer therapy. After lengthy researches and numerous attempts to find the rare pearl, one name came up constantly: Dr R. from Ottawa, Ontario. Getting an appointment was not an easy thing to do as he was booked solid. I had to push and insist that he see Louise as soon as possible: "Her case is serious and urgent," I argued relentlessly. I guess I must have been a good negotiator or a real pain in the neck that one is eager to get rid of, because Dr R. finally agreed to meet with Louise the following week.

First visit to the alternative doctor
Dr R. was a tall, slim cool guy with a full dark-brown beard and he insisted that we call him by his first name. His impressive

résumé detailing his academic and alternative training was available through a brochure in the waiting room. Aside from his medical degree, he had traveled extensively around the world to study with masters and gurus of legendary ancient body-mind-spirit disciplines. After talking shop for a while, as I too was once a licensed naturotherapist, I felt confident of his abilities and knew that we had found the right expert.

The first thing on his agenda was to establish a baseline. Therefore a complete blood works was ordered. Also, he talked to us about chelation therapy and the damage that heavy-metal intoxication can cause to the immune system. Therefore, a special test was also recommended and, of course, both tests involved needles again, a real nightmare for Louise, damn it!

We talked about nutrition, supplements, natural medication and herbs that Louise would have to take as adjuncts to the ten sessions of chelation therapy meant to reduce her body's heavy-metal intoxication level. I thought that going right away with the treatment was a bit premature since we didn't even have the test results yet, but Dr R. seemed to believe that it was a *fait accompli* that, due to our modern way of life, most of us are subject to being contaminated by these kinds of toxins. I reasoned then that in the off chance that he was right, I should ask to take the test also since I needed to remain in top shape for Louise's sake, so I went ahead with the whole shebang. I had read extensively on the subject, and the reports on its safety and efficiency were very positive. Costly treatments by the way, but we considered that the tag of 400 dollars for each test was well worth it; one test before each treatment and one test after each treatment. Double that for me. When it comes to saving one's life, nothing is too expensive.

So here we were a week later for the tests, both patiently sitting side by side in two comfy leather chairs, all hooked up to a drip system similar to the one used for chemotherapy. What differed, though, was that instead of burning chemicals, the liquid running through our veins was laced with some kind of binding agent meant to attract the heavy metals out of our system. Shortly after the infusion was finished, through a urine analysis, our blood's intoxication level would then be determined.

"Through the roof," said the good doctor as he read Louise's test results. The sheet of paper he held in his hands showed a graph detailing a list of heavy metals spread out into a neat column descending on the left side of the page. The level of intoxication was demonstrated by colored lines extending from each name and criss-crossing another set of lines extending downwards that indicated the degree of intoxication. As he pointed with a steady finger to a line in particular, he commented on the fact that all through his career he had only met ten patients with similar results. The red line he was bringing our attention to extended way beyond all the others, so much so that it would have necessitated another whole sheet of paper to capture the full picture. "It's extraordinary that she can swim at all," I said in a stupid attempt to lighten the moment.

Her lead levels were way off the chart and must absolutely be reduced in order to make any significant progress. My test results were high also, but never as dramatic as Louise's. This enlightenment did not really come as bad news to us though, since it represented increased chances of recovery from her cancer once the lead in her body would be removed. At that time we thought that we had found the culprit of Louise's demise and entered into the new battle to come with confidence and renewed hopes. Little did we know that more hardships were yet to come.

January to September, 2009
Louise's CA 125 level goes up again
After the end of the ten sessions, of course another test was required to evaluate the success of our efforts and, yes, it again

involved darn needles. *Poor Louise*, I thought. *I'll have to talk to the staff at the cancer center to try and see if they would have a solution that could help make life a little easier for her.* I felt responsible for her wellbeing, and this stuff about the needles was making me edgy and resentful; something would have to be done soon. As for me, regardless of the results, I had decided not to have more chelation treatments, so the test was unnecessary.

Fifty percent reduction in Louise's heavy-metal level was the result of the latest test. It was very encouraging, but Dr R. thought that, although positive, more reduction was a must and he suggested that Louise go through another round of ten treatments. More needles. *Sh—*, I thought. This came as bittersweet news for Louise, though, who at this stage had not noticed any significant changes in her energy level and seemed to be losing her positive attitude. Not good. The fact also that all these treatments were not covered by Medicare or by our private health insurance was adding to our already high stress level. This venture was getting more costly by the minute; 110 dollars per treatment plus cost of testing and specialized natural medication was beginning to be a heavy burden on our wallets. Now, to top it off, we were considering adding ten more treatments and one more test. Ouch! What the hell? We came this far so we may as well go all the way. If this was to bring my baby back to life, no cost was too high.

But, before going ahead with the second round of treatments, another disturbing situation had to be dealt with: Louise's CA 125 level had gone up again and the gyn-oncologists wanted to see her to talk about more chemo treatments; what a downer. CA 125 is a tumor marker detected through blood tests. When it goes down after treatment, it means that the tumors have shrunk, but when it goes back up again, it may mean that the cancer has come back and it's not an encouraging perspective at this stage of the game, I know something about it.

So here we go again, back to the Ottawa Cancer Centre to

evaluate Louise's condition, and the thought of more chemo treatment was not on our agenda. After a short stay in the waiting room, we're invited by one of the attending nurses to proceed to a private room inside the compound and wait for the specialist on duty. Louise was obviously stressed out and a little depressed and I was impatient and apprehensive at the bad news to come. But we would never in the world have expected to be so shocked by what we were about to hear from Dr F., one of the leading gyn-oncologists in the department. Due to the fact that Louise's CA 125 level had increased, the recurrence of her cancer was suspected. Therefore more chemo was necessary, according to our up-to-now buddy, Dr F. He strongly recommended that Louise go ahead with the treatment as soon as possible. I was nauseated at the mere thought of this and I can only imagine how Louise felt.

After spending some time explaining to us the ins and outs of the treatment, the kind of chemical they use (which was different from the first round of chemo) and the likelihood of side effects, he sat expectantly waiting for us to give him the go-ahead to start the sessions. He was growing more impatient by the minute because of our reluctance to agree. We were considering postponing his treatment in favor of the alternative option. He then stood up suddenly, gathered his paperwork and, exhibiting an air of grandeur, as if we had just insulted him personally, hurriedly proceeded to walk out of the room. Suddenly though, as if his unacceptable behavior was not enough, adding insult to injury, he turned around while crossing the threshold of the door and said with a frustrated voice: "Well, make up your minds quickly before I lose your file in the system."

Even though we were completely taken aback by this poor display of professionalism, we decided not to give in to his undue and unfair pressure and to go ahead with the alternative treatment. Was it a mistake? Time will tell. As for Dr F.'s disappointing behavior, well, I'll let you make up your own mind.

Soon after starting the chelation therapy sessions, we quickly realized that the non-invasive and non-aggressive natural treatments were too slow to kick in compared to the lightning speed at which Louise's cancer was progressing. 'Clear cell ovarian cancer' is very aggressive and the natural treatments could not keep up.

Mental note

Thinking back at times when I feel down, I wonder what motivated us to go ahead with either treatment, natural or chemical. Rationality is not always at the *rendezvous* when lives are threatened. Our survival instinct took over in these confusing times and we somehow always seemed to find the need to overcome the odds. What would an animal do when suffering from a deadly wound? Survive at all cost or lie down and die, realizing instinctively that its time has come? Maybe we should be more like them when we sense that our time may have come, not give in to religious, family or social pressures but let go and face the end of our lives as it comes. In Louise's case, she surprisingly admitted towards the end of her ordeal that she was doing all this partly for me. That she wanted to wipe out the worried look of pain that constantly haunted my eyes every time I looked at her. That she wanted to stick around a little longer to look after me. If only I would have known, I could have told her sooner that it was OK to go: "I'll make it on my own, honey. Even though I'll limp for a while, I'll somehow manage to survive." "Go towards the light, do your thing and stop worrying about me," I would have said, but these words had yet to be offered.

More chemotherapy

Not long after the second chelation therapy treatment was over, tragedy struck again and this time it meant business; ascites were accumulating in her tummy like there was no tomorrow. Ascites is a gastro-enterological accumulation of fluid in the peritoneal cavity. It is a viscous fluid produced by the body to help internal organs slide smoothly on each other, so to speak. The body normally processes and excretes this fluid out of the body by natural means, but sometimes, due to diseases such as liver cirrhosis or cancer, the fluid is not eliminated properly and thus accumulates in the interspaces between the internal organs. The stomach area then swells up progressively, causing a lot of pain and discomfort.

If Louise thought she was afraid of needles before, she hadn't seen anything yet.

Her condition worsened so quickly that we could not wait for her next appointment with the gyn-oncologist, and we had to rush to the Cornwall hospital's emergency to have this monster looked after. The wait was short, thank gawd, and after a quick X-ray of her stomach, the doctor on duty made his diagnostic and arranged to have the fluid removed a.s.a.p. A specialist was needed for this sort of process and they had to fetch one from somewhere in the hospital. Meanwhile, Louise was moved into a small room and the assisting staff prepared her for the procedure. It is then that I saw 'IT' lying on a table by Louise's side: a long and huge curved syringe that looked more like a long narrow siphon, which is what it was actually. It was frightening to look at and in horror I could only guess what it was for.

I can still hear her screams coming out through the closed door as they were inserting, twisting and poking that horrible beast inside her tummy in search of the unwanted liquid. "Sorry, but this had to be done. No choice and no other way; it had to be sucked out," the 'sweating bullets' doctor said later on when it was all over. This moment in time will forever be imprinted in my memory and I wonder if one day I'll be able to recapture it without sorrow and resentment. Time heals all wounds, they say, and I pray it's true for my own wellbeing.

"This liquid will come back as it is due to her cancer and this procedure will have to be repeated," the doctor said, "but we are not equipped here to do this on a regular basis, so you'll have to see your gyn-oncologist for advice."

So, here we go again in a panic and our tails between our legs *en route* for the cancer center to visit our 'not-so-much-our-buddy-anymore' Dr F. the gyn-oncologist, to see what the hell can be done about this situation. As we were waiting nervously, he entered the room swiftly (I thought he had a smirk on his face, but that may just be me), sat on a stool while reading from a bunch of papers he was holding in one hand and mechanically asked Louise to lie down on the examination table. I guess his request must have been just for show, for his exam merely consisted of putting his free hand on her stomach while looking at her and saying condescendingly: "Mrs Milot, when will you understand that this is not going away?", and if I could have read his mind, I'm sure it would have said something like: "Can't you get it into your thick head that you're going to die?"

Well, excuse me for wanting to live, you SOB. What did you think I would do, lie down and die, just like that? Don't I have the right to at least try everything I can to beat this? a teary-eyed Louise later admitted to thinking at that moment.

As a last resort, he offered more chemo (how original), the only intervention possible at this advanced stage according to him. "This is meant to make you more comfortable, you must recognize, not heal you," he said to Louise. When I brought up 'immunotherapy' to his attention as a possible treatment option, he snuffed my comment and brushed it off immediately, saying he didn't know anything about it. "Well," I answered in rebuke, in an effort to stab back at him, "you should visit the Canadian Cancer Society's website. Maybe you would learn a thing or two about it." My feeble retort I have to admit did not even make a dent in his thick hide, but at least it made me feel a tiny bit better; 1 for me, 12 for him.

Why is it that conventional medicine operates with visors and only considers chemotherapy as its sole weapon when it comes to cancer? It seems that it's the only therapy they know or want to know. I've been told over and over again by critics of modern medicine that the almighty dollar motivates its actions. "The humongous 'money-making' pharmaceutical industry is behind all research in that field and lobbies massively to the government to keep it that way," they claim. Even though I am not a strong believer in conspiracy theories, I sometimes wonder about the veracity of these sayings. There are numerous other fields in which research could be done: alternative medicine, nutrition, immunotherapy and especially psychosomatics which promote the concept that our emotions could be responsible for our physical demise or wellbeing. Why not investigate there for a change? But noooo, these natural approaches do not bring in enough 'bacon' to the massive money-making pharmaceutical industry and are therefore of no interest, are slipped under the carpet and forgotten in file 13. I for one have decided to put a hold on my donations to cancer research until I see a serious change of attitude in that field.

Coming back to us, the situation was so dramatic and pressing that we did not have any other choice but to go ahead with another round of chemo in an effort to eliminate the ascites. In our heads, though, this was a temporary solution and we were going back to complete the chelation therapy sessions. Both therapies were going to be given in the same span of time, even though in different locations, and the needle problem became even more evident; a solution had to be found and it came in the form of a 'PIC' line. It was Chinese to me when I first heard the name, but the concept made a lot of sense after a few explanations. A 'peripherally inserted central catheter' (PICC or PIC line) is a form of intravenous access that can be used for a prolonged period of time or long chemotherapy regimens or extended antibiotic therapy. It is inserted in a peripheral vein and advanced through increasingly larger veins, toward the heart.

The tube is neatly rolled up under the arm and held in place with medical-grade adhesive tape until it is needed. At each session, it is unrolled and the needle through which flows the treatment liquid is inserted into the soft connector at the end of the tube instead of into the patient's skin.

After Louise gratefully accepted the offer to install the PIC line, arrangements were made and it was to be installed on the same day as her first chemo treatment would start. Energy-wise, it was a bit much for her, I thought, but it was well worth it. Also the fact that the same PIC line could be used for the chelation therapy was an added benefit. I was very glad and relieved for Louise as it would render her treatment so much more tolerable. Bravo for modern technology.

Soon after her sessions began though, another complication arose: the chemo was not eliminating the ascites fast enough and Louise was suffering, more than a little I might add. Something had to be done, and fast. Modern technology was once more solicited and came to the rescue successfully. An 'AbdominX' was inserted to help evacuate the ascites from Louise's tummy without the use of that awful, almost medieval torture apparatus previously used in the emergency room. Thank God for that.

Normally used to drain fluids from the lungs of cancer patients, then called a 'PleurX', the unit had been adapted to suck the ascites from the stomach area and it was doing a great job. It consisted again of a tube (but larger than the one used for the PIC line) that was inserted through the stomach lining and went directly into the areas where the ascites lay. Twice a week at first, a nurse would come to our home to drain the fluid from Louise's stomach. Over the weeks, the chemo did its work; the ascites level went down so much that the drainage had to be done only once a week and was eventually stopped as Louise's condition finally stabilized. After she was feeling better, I could not restrain myself from joking about the fact that I thought she looked like a creature from outer space with all these wires coming out of her body; a few more springs and a metal cap on her head and, *voilà*, your perfect ET. She was a good sport about it and didn't mind my juvenile poking as it acted as an efficient stress-buster for us. All through this period, a zillion things happened and I'd go nuts trying to detail them all. Suffice it to say that Louise was in a period of remission and we were on an upswing. Of course there were the occasional little blips like when she had to be rehydrated. Picture this: Louise was already wired up with a PIC line rolled up and taped under her armpit, an 'AbdominX' rolled up and taped on her stomach, and now she had to sit, lie and walk around to her numerous appointments with some kind of battery-operated pump containing a rehydrating solution that was shot through her veins with the help of more tubes and needles stuck in her hand (the PIC line could not be used on this one). The whole damn apparatus was hanging inconveniently by her side on a strap looped around her shoulder and had to be removed and repositioned each time she got dressed or had to put on that ridiculous 'try-to-not-show-your-ass' hospital gown before each test, and there were more than a few, trust me! I tell you, she looked like a zombie out of a scary movie, and if the situation was not so serious, it would have been hilarious.

But aside from those little bumps in the road, things were good and both the chelation and chemotherapy treatments were following their course smoothly. The side effects from the chemo, blisters between Louise's fingers and ulcers in her mouth, were minimal and somewhat manageable without too much discomfort. Of course, she lost her hair a second time and head scarves were once more in fashion. It was a busy period traveling several times a week to Ottawa for two different treatments, but her energy was increasing by the weeks and we felt more and more confident that we could beat the monster.

Louise always had this dream about owning a knitting-wool store and since she was doing so well with her treatments, I decided to support her and do everything I could to help put the project together. After preparing a simple and easy business and marketing plan, I set out to convert the country kitchen of our small house into a cute little store and ordered the required products for sale. I even modified our wrap-around veranda in a way that she could exhibit her merchandise outside during the weekends. We called it 'The Store on a Porch.' It looked great, inviting, held good promises of success, and Louise was happy which was worth a million dollars to me. *Will she be able to enjoy it a long time though?* I questioned and I truly hoped that the feeling of dread rattling my guts was just a figment of my imagination.

October 9, 2009

The cancer is gone...for now

Louise and I were sitting nervously on one of the comfy leather couches spread out neatly in the huge hall of the 'Critical Care Building' adjacent to the Ottawa Hospital's Cancer Centre. My hands were shaking with anticipation as I prepared to read Louise's latest scan report we had just picked up at the administration office. The look I gave her after perusing the results said it all, and with happy smiling faces we jumped up with joy and 'high fived' the moment; no more traces of cancer could be detected!

Little did we know then that sadly this marked the beginning of the end.

Chapter 9

Post-Loss:
May to August 2011
Anger, depression, boredom
Letting go of old attachments, creating a new identity,
reinventing myself, redirecting released energies towards
new goals

My crushing loneliness

Although acting out my pain with my new toy brings some momentary relief, making a fool of myself by driving my Caddie like a maniac is not going to solve the issue and can only get me into deep trouble. The loneliness and the boredom I feel is profoundly rooted and although I have come a long way in positively managing my grief, it is still not over and I feel help is needed. Well, not help, I prefer the word 'support.' My sick sense of independence will not allow me to break down and ask for help; I don't know, I've always been like that, it's a thing with me. Another damn issue I'll have to work on eventually.

I have never been a social beast, as they say; I'm more of the semi-loner type sitting by myself in a corner observing people going on about their business. So joining social groups and the likes does not appeal to me. A therapist? Whoa! The mere thought of it gives me the creeps. My ego will not suffer it, no dice. Then, as I am cogitating on the matter, the word 'BFO' comes to mind. I remember reading about the Bereaved Families of Ontario, a non-profit organization dedicated to supporting grieving people who are going through the difficult period of losing a loved one. I make arrangements to meet with them. This turns out to be one of the best moves I ever made.

My first contact with the grieving group

The place is small, the atmosphere warm and friendly. E., the coordinator, makes me feel at ease and seems to understand my grief instantly, even just after a short talk upon my arrival. What a relief. I am then invited to join one of their many support groups which consist of people sitting in a circle around a facilitator whose task is to encourage the participants to express their feelings about their losses. I am so enthusiastic about the whole process that I decide on the spot to become a volunteer facilitator myself. Not everyone can become a facilitator of course and I have to fill out a bunch of forms and pass an interview to evaluate if I fit the psychological profile required to take on this challenging task. I receive a passing grade and I am scheduled for the next training course that is to take place in the following spring. Meanwhile, part of my education will be to attend the support groups a couple of times a month, which will at the same time offer me the support I need. I leave the place with a good feeling and enjoy a short reprieve from the stabbing knife in my guts.

As I drive back home to my empty house, my mind is still occupied by the details and the impressions that the place left on me. Aside from the courtesy and the genuine compassion I felt from the staff, what struck me the most is the massive amount of flyers, pamphlets and books on grieving that they have available for borrowing. Impressive. They range from grieving the loss of a child, a parent, a sibling, a spouse, to loss by suicide. They even have a substantial array of literature covering the loss of a pet...hum, a pet, that brings me back to my old buddy, Max.

I've been thinking a lot about the little guy since I'm alone and it stirs a lot of mixed emotions. How could I not? He's the only living being in my house right now, heck in my immediate life...But he's getting old and I can read the signs everywhere; his ears are shot and he bumps into things as he is slowly losing his vision. His sight is not the only thing going either; his mind is too, I suspect. The loss of Louise was very hard on him also and it left a noticeable mark. The other day, in a fit of confusion, he started running towards my neighbor thinking he was me (or maybe Louise) while I was just standing there by his side. I kept calling him back to no avail, and in the end I had to run like a madman to go get him, for I was afraid he would get hit by a car. Dammit, I'm too old for this.

His hind legs are weak and he's incontinent, which is a real pain in the ass. Picking up pee and poop on the floor is not my idea of fun. But I love him, always did, always will, no matter what. Since the very first moment I held this cute soft black silky fur puppy in my arms as he was joyfully licking my ears, I felt I could never part from him.

I know the time will come when I'll have to do the right thing, but for now, the medication I give him seems to keep the suffering at bay, so I'll hold off on that decision, maybe a month, six months, a year. Who knows? I'll be inspired when the moment comes. Am I doing it for him or for me? Mostly for me, I guess, as I feel I could not endure another heavy loss in my life right now. "So it will be diapers for you, buddy, like it or not; pale blue diapers, that is. Ya, ya, we know it's embarrassing and we hope there are no females around to make fun of you while we parade in that ridiculous accoutrement. Hey, old pal," I tell him while he looks at me with his half-open watery tired eyes, "it's the only color they had, buddy, sorry."

"Hey, you dog diaper makers," I say out loud, "what the heck are you thinking? Couldn't you make a better effort and at least offer black and white products to fit most dog colors? Who's ever heard of a blue freaking dog? Wake up, guys." Anyway, a page is turned, life goes on and 'blue diaper wearing Max' and I try to make the best of every new day as more challenges await us at each corner.

Music in the grieving process: a Zen moment

'April showers bring May flowers,' they used to say, but nowadays it is rather: 'May showers bring June flowers,' and the dismal weather does not help my grief. Today is another darn rainy Monday and I'm sitting in front of my computer screen lazily reading my e-mails. I'm in no particular mood, if not a little bored like the weather, and I look for things to do later on in the day. As I distractedly listen to Michael Bublé's warm velvety voice coming through my PC's speakers rendering his version of 'The Way You Look Tonight,' I tap my foot on the floor to the cool sensual bossa-nova beat, and I give in to the idea that it could not be such a bad day after all. Then suddenly, out of nowhere, totally unexpectedly, like an explosion, an image of Louise's dying face pops up in my mind and I'm instantly engulfed in a kaleidoscope of raw and painful memories of the dreadful day when she left me. At once, my world is unequivocally turned upside down. The damn roller-coaster ride is back again. Crap.

I feel invisible, clawing hands creeping inside my chest, encroaching on my heart like a monster's tentacles, while, with a piercing stomach jab, the unmistakable signs of grief reappear. Not fighting it, as I know darn well that there is no evading grief, I decide to rough it out, stretch back on my director's chair, punch the media player's repeat button, rest my head, close my eyes and allow the music to do its cleansing magic.

Surrendering to the beautiful melody, I experience only conflict though, for where there should be soothing tenderness, there is only growing hurt and sorrow, every musical note a stabbing blade, every word an aching memory.

As the song keeps playing over and over, I begin to feel the music seeping in through every fiber of my being, vibrating at my very core, digging in deeper and deeper into my pain, and I weep. There seems to be no end to the liberating tears rolling down my cheeks and I don't even bother to wipe them as they abundantly run along my neck to soak the collar of my shirt. But as time passes by, a transition occurs and progressively music becomes only music, words become only words, the weeping finally subsides, and I recapture some kind of composure. *Maybe there'll be flowers in June*, I hope.

Reinventing myself

Enough of the mushy stuff, no more tears. If the June flowers don't come early enough, then I'll go and get the freaking flowers myself. In a fit of revolt, I jump into my car and head to downtown Montreal to cruise in the shopping malls.

As I slowly drive west on Highway 401 in my shiny Caddie, I plan my day; first it will be a nice fedora, then a suit complete with all the fuss that goes with it, and to finish, a special little *gâterie* I haven't had for a long time. I'm not sure if this will really help restore my messed-up sense of self, but it will at least be fun for a change. 'Here and now is all we have,' remember?

In an all-afternoon shopping spree, my mission is accomplished sooner than expected; the hat is a genuine gorgeous black Borsalino I bought at Henri & Henri, a reputed Montreal hat boutique. Apparently, a few days earlier, Charlie Sheen, the Hollywood actor, had bought the same model, except he purchased a dozen while I walked away with only one, but I'm happy anyway and a little flattered that a celebrity has the same taste in hats as I do.

From the Hugo Boss collection in the Saint Catherine Street Bay store, I spoil myself with a fabulous fine summer wool black suit, a crisp white dress shirt, a stylish grey tie, a black leather belt, socks and a superb pair of black Italian soft leather shoes, all marketed by the same designer. From the fragrance and toiletries concessions on the ground floor, I let myself be seduced by the enchanting scent of a Ralph Lauren Polo Double Black cologne that I acquire on the spot. I feel content and satisfied, at least for now. The bill? Well, you don't want to know and I hope I won't feel a little silly for having spent all that cash later on when I think back on my little escapade, but if tomorrow I wake up still feeling crummy and in the dumps, then at least I'll look great in my new threads and I'll smell like Prince Charming.

Now on to my next little treat. As I exit the store I'm like a predator sniffing its prey. It's a beautiful sunny day and even though I'm lost in a sea of humanity going about its business and a massive traffic jam with restless car drivers honking impatiently, it is not exhaust fumes I smell, but the fresh invigo-rating air of spring (it must be in my head, but who cares). I'm happy...and hungry! My antennas are widely deployed as I'm magnetically attracted towards my destination. I can only think of one thing: food! With determined steps, holding the couple of plastic bags containing my take of the day, I eagerly make my way on Saint Catherine Street, barely paying attention to the massive amount of retail stores crowding the avenue. Even the attractive girls showing off their new spring wardrobe and their sexy legs do not deter me from my mission. Well, a little, but my quest for grub is stronger for now. My stomach is growling and I start to salivate the minute I turn left on the corner of Metcalfe Street. A few steps more and there it is, right across the street from Dominion Park, the famous Dunn's Delicatessen, the best smoked-meat joint in town. Yummy! What a feast this will be. I anticipate the best as the waitress deposits the sinful food in front of me. An abnormally invitingly large smoked-meat sandwich, a generously salted and vinegared order of fat fries and a coke, all the elements of a healthy meal for a growing boy. Awesome. With greasy fingers, I gulp the whole thing like a pig and to hell with clogged arteries and tight pant belts. Never did a meal taste that great. A good day.

Grief creeps up on me

In spite of my little *sorties*, my days are still boringly long and the loneliness I feel seems to have taken permanent residency in my being. So in an effort to pull out of my rut, I decide to renovate the kitchen of my little house, something I've been meaning to do for some time now but I kept putting off, I know why now. At first when Louise passed away, I could not get rid of her possessions fast enough as I couldn't bear the sight of them, too painful. But now that I have matured in my grief, it seems to be the contrary that takes place and there are certain things I tend to hang on to. Most unfortunate also is the fact that I occasionally regret having parted with a certain object too swiftly.

The old kitchen for instance is one of those things I have a hard time to let go of; the old faded, scratched and full-of-nail-holes paneled walls, the tired warped cabinet doors, the bumpy arborite-covered counter that had over the years become unglued and the yellowed square floor tiles now all remind me affectionately of Louise and the countless hours we spent together in that room. The hopes and despair, the good and bad days we shared together all through her journey. I'm hesitant to part from that now, which is silly, actually; memories are in my heart, not in a physical place. Still, I hung on. But I must not let this deter me from going on with my quest for the new me; I must be strong, go forward and work hard at it.

Over the weeks as renovation progresses and the old kitchen slowly becomes a thing of the past, similar instances of sad reminiscences occur and intrude upon my busy mind. One of them is particularly difficult and I wish I could turn back the clock to undo what I now think was a mistake on my part.

Pressing that delete key too fast

The incident occurred some days ago as I was working on my computer. For some reason I needed a USB memory stick and I set out to pick one randomly from the many lying on my desk. As I inserted the unit in the USB slot on the computer, the display screen showed that it still contained a bunch of files I thought I had erased (earlier). Curious, I started to open them up and to my greatest surprise I agonizingly realized that they contained all kinds of pictures of Louise and of us together, letters and private little notes that she had made to herself during the period she was sick. As I read hesitantly, I could not help but feel as if I was intruding on her privacy. I felt as if I was borrowing her desk while she walked out of the room to fetch a coffee or something. At that precise moment, she took life once more. As fast as it had arrived, the feeling evaporated and reality set in: she's gone and will never come back. I was engulfed by an overwhelming feeling of emptiness and sadness again. Overwhelmed by grief once more and almost in a panic, I started to delete the files rapidly.

I could not press the delete button fast enough as I was eager to end my suffering as fast as I could. But my damn curiosity was getting the better of me and, in spite of my emotional turmoil, I had to, ever so discreetly, watch with my peripheral vision the little window popping up at the bottom left of the screen showing the content of the files being deleted. Click, watch, delete, click, watch, delete. It went on like this for a while until one particular window caught my eye. It was the picture of a slightly intoxicated Louise wearing a baseball cap all askew, like teenagers often do, and showing a tired but content smile. She was looking straight at me with her penetrating eyes and was cheering happily while waving a glass of wine towards my camera. I had taken the picture after a little party we had to celebrate one of her recurring periods of remission. I was tempted to keep it, but after some deliberations, I decided that it was too close to the mark and, with an uncertain trembling finger, I hit the delete key.

It was only when I woke up the next morning that I realized my error and, with a sorry heart, I rushed to the computer to try and recuperate the document. Too late, everything was gone; even the trash file was empty as I had, in my usual efficient manner, also deleted any folders or subfolders in which the file might have still existed. In my haste to keep my grieving pain at bay, I had destroyed one of the few remaining worthwhile memorabilia left of Louise. I could have cherished it forever and now it was just a memory that will in time sadly fade away. Will it really though? Does the mental image of a strong meaningful moment ever disappear? Who knows? Only time will tell. *Anyway,* I thought, *I still have four crates full of pictures of 38 years of family life stored in the basement to sort out.* That will be a job for later though, much later.

Little did I know then that there could have been a slight possibility of retrieving the photo by restoring my computer to a previous date as apparently files are never completely erased from a computer. But by the time I learned about this little trick, an infuriating incident had occurred, making this bright idea an impossibility: the computer's motherboard and hard drive died on me, but more about this later.

Keeping the boredom at bay

My life now can only be described as humdrum. It seems these days that everything I do is meaningless, everywhere I go is boring, everyone I meet is uninteresting. It must be a phase I'm going through, I guess, as I remember very well having had some good times here and there before, even though they never lasted very long, I was still on a high then and it felt good, but now...Granted, I don't feel like slitting my throat every other day anymore, which could mark an improvement, but still. Why can't I get out of this stupid rut I'm in? Dammit.

For instance, just yesterday, I visited my little sister, and no sooner had I walked through the door than I wanted to rush out again. No fault of hers, mind you. Ginette is a darling; it's just me that's messed up. On another occasion, I go to meet my older brother that I hadn't seen for a lifetime; same damn thing. I say hello, hang around for an excruciating 30 minutes, and I can't wait to zoom out of there, like a bat out of hell.

I just can't help it, I feel weird and lost all the time; I'm not happy when I'm alone and I'm miserable in the company of others. Actually, at the moment, I can't stand the company of others, even though there's a small part of me that somehow wants to connect. I keep giving in to an extremely uncomfortable restlessness. I seem to be enslaved by a constant frantic search for solace. I'm so confused and disoriented it's not even funny. I'm caught in a Catch 22, an inescapable loop; I go places, I do things, I see people, I get bored, I leave and find myself alone again and miserable,f... I feel like the darn Energizer battery bunny zipping around aimlessly, banging my face into walls and returning to the middle again...lost, desperate and in search mode once more. The knot in my stomach keeps getting tighter, choking me; what an awful feeling.

This has got to change, I say to myself one day as I'm in an upswing. I repeat my mantra to get a life or you're done, man; you need to kick your sorry ass and pull yourself out of that crazy hole you're stuck in. In the end, my efforts reap some rewards and, remembering how good I felt after my little *sortie* in Montreal, I decide to take off for Toronto, the big city, to visit my friends and hang around downtown. Maybe that'll perk me up a little bit.

As I'm heading west on Highway 401, I turn on my car phone (voice activated, 'thank you') and I book myself a nice room at the Royal York, one of the most luxurious hotels in Toronto. I probably shouldn't spend all that money, but escaping the brutal pains of grief gives me all the best excuses in the world.

Spending the afternoon walking the busy streets and shopping till I drop (didn't buy a thing this time) does not seem to appease the angry gods of grief and I return to my *casa*, deflated. Not ready to face the eeriness of an empty hotel room, like a zombie I wander aimlessly in the enormous lobby, totally unappreciative of its splendor and of the numerous glamorous shops and boutiques contained in it. After eating a tasteless meal that would have been otherwise a feast for anyone else, I crash lifelessly on one of the foyer's soft leather couches and get busy sipping a Scotch, trying unsuccessfully to lose myself in the buzz of things around me. I feel more alone than ever. This is not working. Being alone sucks big time. I'm still missing Louise tremendously and I wonder desperately if that'll ever change. When she passed away, a large part of me went with her. I feel like a wounded bird missing a wing. How can I ever fly again? Hum...I fear it'll take more than a double Scotch to get me into Morpheus's arms tonight.

The next day is not any better and, even in the company of my long-time friends whom I love dearly, I've got the jitters and feel compelled to say my goodbyes and take off like a scared cat after only a few hours' visit. Totally messed up, I hurry back to check out of my hotel sooner than expected and zoom out of town feeling defeated, sad and discouraged. I'm coming back home and the desperate loop goes on.

This rotten mood of mine seems to be never-ending. I can't seem to find enjoyment in anything I do and I remain in an exhausting search mode. It's like on the one hand I'm totally disinterested in life itself, but on the other I'm haunted by an existential need to fight my way through the storm and find a port to dock.

Going to parties, movies, BBQs or visiting fairs doesn't cut it. I'm still lost and indifferent to the core and I need something or someone that will positively impact my existence sufficiently to give me the boost I need to help me rise from the ashes of my loss. Unbeknown to me at this time though, the stage is being set for me to cross paths with the person who's about to change my life.

My first brush with Christine

The Glengarry Highland Games are just as monotonous as all the other events I've attended lately, and I hope my Scottish friends won't take offense at my comment; it's just me. The day is horribly hot, dry and the fairgrounds suffocatingly packed to capacity. The air is filled with the constant underlying nasal sound of bagpipes as there are isolated groups of bagpipers practicing everywhere on the grounds. The cacophony it creates is almost unbearable for my untrained ear, and, disappointed, I leave in a hurry after just a short visit.

But that day left an impression on me, as I realize upon awakening this morning. I just can't put my finger on it and, differently from all the other times, the memory of that day sticks with me. I experience a vague and confusingly pleasant feeling suggesting to me that there's been a slight shift in my emotional state. It's nothing like I've ever experienced before and I like it. Is this the light at the end of the tunnel?

I will learn soon enough why this is so though, as, after meeting Christine, she'll surprisingly confirm to me that she was there on that particular day. Maybe we exchanged a brief glance as we walked through the narrow aisles or stood close to each other while visiting the same booth. Maybe we were not even physically present in the same time and space and I somehow psychically picked up her essence and sensed the energies of occurrences meant to be. Synchronicity, serendipity? Who knows? Life is full of surprises, but I think that this particular moment in time was a turning point in my life. Am I right? Only time will tell, and meanwhile, even though life tastes a little sweeter this morning, I am still caught up in an exhausting uphill battle and I'm haunted by the daunting task ahead.

Scattering Louise's ashes

It's been on my mind for a while now, but I keep putting it off. I'm usually not a procrastinator, but this is beyond what I ever did before. I keep saying that I'm waiting for the perfect day, but I know it's just an excuse. The thought of touching Louise's remains is nothing less than horrifying and I resent the moment I'm going to have to do it, or is it just another excuse to hang on to her?

Dammit, I'm going to have to do it, I promised her, I think while looking at the expectant urn. With resignation, I acknowledge that today is the day, the stage is perfect; the sun is shining bright and high, a warm, gentle breeze caresses my skin softly, and my fully blooming spirea shows off a gorgeous coat of magnificent white flowers that looks as if a lazy snow had gently fallen upon them.

I could not pick a better time to honor Louise's memory and so, with dread, I pick up the urn sitting by her picture on an old wooden shelf in the country kitchen, ready to do the necessary thing. I get to work quickly. This is so creepy, I can't believe I'm doing this. I pick up the scary ossuary, unscrew its top, pull out the secured bag containing the ashes and empty its contents in a coverless box large enough to stick my hand into. I rush out the door to do the deed as soon as possible. It was an arrangement we had together; no fuss, no ceremony, our little thing. I was to do this for her, and her for me, had I gone first.

Carrying my precious cargo, I start by walking to our favorite spot by the riverside under the impressive weeping willow tree hanging over rows of overgrown water weeds. Standing under its comforting canopy, I pause a minute and take a deep breath, inhaling the pungent scent of decaying vegetation crushed under my feet. I stare at the container with trepidation and, after a brief hesitation, with an uncertain hand I dig into the box and scoop up a handful of ashes. It feels gritty like coarse sand and still contains tiny fragments of bones that had not been completely burned away. The macabre sensation of touching Louise's last remains is very disturbing and I quickly dispose of the troubling dust by spreading it into the air and over the slow flowing waters of the lazy Raisin River. "Farewell, honey, I'll miss you forever," I say to myself and, with teary eyes, I move on. I repeat the same scenario at different spots in the backyard that were significant to her; the bird-house sitting area, the wild flower field, and I finish up by the Japanese white lilac tree I had just planted in her memory.

Life's twisted sense of humor has no boundaries and can sometimes interfere comically in the sanctity of the most revered moments.

At some point during my little ritual, a sudden gust of wind caught me by surprise and blew the ashes back into my eyes. Half blinded and waving wildly an inquiring hand in front of me trying to get my bearings, I stupidly walked into the entangled branches of my crab-apple tree and almost dropped the container with the remaining ashes as I rushed back out away from the angry wasps nesting in there.

The situation was so ridiculous that I have to laugh at myself. Aside from my red irritated eyeballs and the itchy stings in my face and butt, I feel surprisingly good and cool about spreading Louise's ashes, something I was not expecting. I thought it would have been harder. Little did I know then that it was not to be so for long and that another storm was gathering.

Empowered by my newfound sense of accomplishment, I decide to take advantage of the rest of this beautiful day to do a little gardening around the house. Most of my time in the yard is somehow enjoyable, which is a surprise to me. However, I get into trouble the minute I start setting up the flower baskets hung outside my wrap-around screened-in porch, as I am overwhelmed by a powerful wave of melancholy; this had always been Louise's job, and even in sickness she did it perfectly. The baskets were always splendid. *How can I even come close to her artwork?* I think. With soiled hands planted awkwardly in the black earth of one of the baskets, I try my best, but I feel inadequate, out of place and sad. I drop everything, walk into the house hurriedly and get busy at making dinner.

Still on a streak, after a reasonably acceptable steak dinner and a glass of French red wine, I decide to move my electronic piano from the cluttered country kitchen to my study where it would be more accessible should I decide to tickle its black and white keys, something that I haven't done for a lifetime, it seems.

Giving in to the natural artistic instincts that holding the instrument awakens in me, I can't resist the urge to give it a try. I set it up on its stand, plug it in, push the start button, sit down on the assorted black leather bench and get ready to play. Before starting, I close my eyes and inhale deeply as I sensually lay my fingers on the keys and allow the music to come to life. It's like magic, and no matter how long I've been away from it, it's still there: the music, my lifesaver, my lifetime companion, my drug. At first it seems like an effort to reach inside as there is so much pain in there, but soon, in a trained response, the music starts to flow and the melodies take form like blooming flowers.

I tirelessly go from one romantic song to another as I progressively recapture my long-lost dexterity, when all of a sudden all hell breaks loose. Immediately after playing the first melancholic chords of Barry Manilow's song, 'This One's for You,' I know I'm in trouble. Like a true artist, I play with great emotional intensity, each musical note resonates in me like a sounding board, and I easily slip into the passion that the composer meant to express in the song. This time it's no different and I lose myself in a kaleidoscope of poignant and painful feelings as I associate the meaning of the words with my own life. I then break down in tears and the world becomes silent again save for the soft sound of my irrepressible sobs.

I recognize that playing that song triggered the sensations I should have expressed this morning, but it's more, much more than that. I suddenly understand that scattering Louise's ashes represents another step forward in my quest to let go of my last attachments to her. I come to grips with the fact that keeping her last remains close to me acted as a crutch that kept me limping instead of walking. I had this silly notion that Louise faithfully stood there watching over me. It was comforting, but not healthy. The level of emotional release brought upon by my extraordinary musical interlude expresses the finality of her departure;

she is gone forever, a pitiful and painful reality I must face. I have to stand tall and walk alone from now on.

Managing my frustrations

The past weeks have been tarred with weird, frustrating and inexplicable incidents. First it was the watches. After hearing the details, tell me that there is not some kind of paranormal phenomenon at play here. I have three watches and they have always worked perfectly well. One morning, two weeks ago, I got up, dressed and, as I was getting ready to put on my old Timex wristwatch, I noticed that it had stopped. Thinking that it needed a new battery, I take it to Sears to have a new one put in. I leave it with the repairman while I go shopping for half an hour. Upon my return, I learn from him that the battery is good but that the watch is broken. "Leave it here and I will fix it for you," he says, and I accept.

I then go home to fetch my nice Simon Chang watch, put it on proudly and go on with my business. It's not half an hour that I'm wearing it when I notice with consternation that it has stopped also. In frustration I growl to myself, *What the hell is going on?* Here I go again, back to see Mr 'Watch Repairman' to change the battery. This time I wait while he fiddles with it, but the wait is short. "Sir, your battery is good, it's the watch that's broken," he says with a puzzled look on his face. More and more put off by this silly situation, I leave the watch for repair, thinking that I will try the gold pocket watch that Louise gave me later when I get back home.

The following day, I fumble through my jewelry box to see where the heck I buried that gold watch so I can hang it on my belt. *It's the last one I have, hope it works,* I think. After reading with melancholy the inscription on the inside cover ('I love you, Louise'), I crank it a few times and it starts right away to my greatest delight. Tell me that you have an idea of what happened next? Right, you guessed it. After wearing the thing for a short while it also stopped dead in its tracks. Weird, isn't it? Know that to date, while the two other watches regained life under the magical touch of my new buddy the watch fixer, the needles of Louise's gift to me still remain frozen in time.

Now, listen to this one; it's even weirder. Louise had two nice watches that I kept in her jewelry box, hidden in a closet. Although I got rid of most of her possessions, I kept all her rings, earrings, bracelets, pins and watches as I thought they would make nice anniversary gifts for my daughter and grand-daughters. Following the bizarre occurrences that happened with my watches, I got curious about Louise's so I decided to see if they had suffered the same fate. After opening the dark wooden box, I found them immediately; they sat in a segregated compartment, waiting to ornate a wrist that would never come back.

In spite of a few pinches in my heart at the sight of all the sparkling paraphernalia that were once dear to Louise, I go on. I pick up the two watches and let them hang around my index and second fingers with the dial facing me. I look at them, remembering with sorrow the times when she would dress up and put them on proudly. But as I take a closer look at the clocks, I freeze in consternation: both watches had stopped at the exact same time. Furthermore, the needles indicating the seconds were also frozen at the exact same second. Whoa! What do you think of that? Bizarre, isn't it? And to date, I still don't have a rational explanation; a message from the other side?

That was the weird part; now on to the frustration build-up. As I said before, I own a computer, well actually, it was Louise's, and it always performed perfectly, until the dreaded day. I had been working on it for some time when suddenly, a huge X appeared on my screen. It was colored a bright red on a black background, very impressive, I can tell you that. Completely taken aback, I flipped buttons here and there and wildly jiggled my mouse to no avail. The thing was gone. Dead. *Kaput.* After an hour or more messing around with wires and all sorts of connections, in a fit of deep irritation I unplug the freaking thing, grab it under my arm and take off to see Mr Computer Repair Guy this time.

After a quick examination, the verdict is solid. "Your motherboard is completely fried. You have to get a new computer," the technician droned. "I can transfer the content of your hard drive into the new computer if you wish," he furthered, trying to appease my evident mounting exasperation. So it went. I bought a brand-new machine with all the gizmos, had the content of my old hard drive transferred into it, reluctantly paid the cashier and took off for home.

Everyone who's ever bought a new computer knows that it's a big pain in the butt, as you have to reactivate all your programs, key in all your passwords, and get acquainted with the environment of your new toy, etc., etc. All and all, doing this took me roughly the better half of Friday and Saturday. Exhausted, I logged out and said my goodbyes to Mr Acer. See you Monday, my new friend, and I took off for the rest of the weekend.

Ah, Monday, a brand-new day alone with my newly acquired trinket. *Let's forget about what happened before and concentrate on what's coming*, I think happily. I sit down at my desk, push the 'on' button on the machine and wait, wait, and wait for the screen to light up. With rising anxiety, I wiggle my mouse, gently tap the desktop unit and still nothing. I shut off my 'not-so-much-my-new-friend-anymore' gizmo to see if that would change anything, but still no life in the damn thing. "Fuzz," I say out loud with stretched lips and grinding teeth, and just as I am about to lose it, letters start to appear on the black screen. *Finally!* I think with relief, and I start to read.

As the words form in my head, relief turns into surprise, surprise turns into amazement, amazement turns into incredulity and incredulity into anger when the meaning of the infuriating little message posted on the screen strikes me. "You are about to lose all the content of your memory, please close your computer immediately and contact your dealer as soon as possible." I am awestruck and dumbfounded and with 'jaw-dropping' consternation, I shut the bastard off, almost rip the connections off the wall, grab the @#* thing...And take off for the freaking store...again.

Mr Computer Guy cannot believe his eyes when he sees me whiz into the store like a madman on a mission. "I've been in the business for years, sir, and I have never ever seen this happen before," he apologizes (*You must be the unluckiest son-of-a-bitch I know*, I'm thinking he must be thinking right now but is too chicken to say so in front of his 'fire-shooting-from-his-eyeballs' client). Here we go again. Same scenario as before: evaluation, prognostic (motherboard fried), purchase, transfer of hard drive content, and trip back home. "Another two darn days ahead messing around with this s—" I gripe as I park my car in the driveway. This stuff is true. I'm telling you, it really happened; I'm not making this up, but wait...there's more.

Holding on tight to my precious package, I climb up the stairs to the veranda, open the screen door and, as I am ready to put my keys in the lock, I see it on the floor: the new Yellow Pages phonebook has arrived. I can finally see what my new ad on stress management looks like (I had just newly reopened my practice). I pick it up, open the door, deposit the computer box gently on the floor and, still barely containing my 'post-traumatic stress' and just about ready to call myself up for a consultation, I peruse the ad and realize with disbelief that they have put in the wrong phone number... "Aaaargh!" I scream at the top of my lungs, and I miserably have to admit that, at this stage, the Webster dictionary did not contain enough dialogue to describe my feelings and there were way too few swearwords to express my revolt.

A bath of anger

I command myself to hold on after a few mini clouds of angry fumes puff out of my ears announcing an incoming volcano. "Take a few deep breaths and control yourself, man," I repeat over and over. With clenched teeth, I lay down the phonebook on the kitchen table with a show of exaggerated delicateness, walk straight to the living room and reach for my faithful buddy Mr Scotch. I fill half of one of my 'old fashion' crystal glasses with it, climb upstairs to the bathroom and start running myself a hot bath. There, this should mellow me down a bit before I call the phone company to let it all out and rip someone apart. I start sipping the burning liquid as I undress, waiting for the tub to fill up.

Soon, the soothing alcohol does its job and my stomach starts to relax as I slip into the hot water. As a therapist, I was aware of the powerful emotional cleansing effect of a hot bath on a stressed person, but I never experienced it myself...until now. I have two things working for me (or against me, depending on how you look at it): the hot bath helping my repressed emotions bubble up and the alcohol inhibiting my intellect and eradicating all sense of control in me, a nasty combination. The storm has gathered and pandemonium breaks loose.

There are several stages of anger according to psychology. It can go from simple annoyance to frustration, infuriation and hostility to downright raging fury. At this moment, mine tips at the end of the scale and I dangerously need an outlet. The annoyances and frustrations of the past few weeks are just the tip of the iceberg and pale in comparison with the underlying cesspool of suppressed emotions hiding in my gut. Three years of fear, guilt, helplessness, resentfulness, and desperation have cumulated into a massive thunderstorm and they're knocking at my door. The watches, the computers, and the Yellow Pages incidents are just the triggers I need. Suddenly thunder roars angrily in the air and furious lightning sparks hit the ground.

Lying in the hot water, I scream out loud until my throat

hurts, I huff and puff and hyperventilate like a moron, I thrash the water with my hands and feet, making a huge mess of the whole bathroom. I swear to God, the hospital staff and the doctors for failing Louise and me. I yell my resentfulness at Louise for being sick, dying and leaving me alone, and I cry for all the times I didn't cry and should have. The feeling of guilt I experience for not being able to do more to help Louise and for feeling impatient with her at times during her ordeal is more than a little disturbing and I realize in the end that most of my anger is directed at me. Will I ever be able to forgive myself?

Although short, my violent outburst is extremely liberating, and soon after completing a few cleansing breath exercises, I'm able to just lie there motionless, spent, and a bit confused as to where my life is going from now on. *Here and now is all I have and I must make the best of it*, I force myself to believe as I get out of the bathtub, dry off, dress and get ready to face the world once more.

Cleaning up the family pictures

Wait a year, the grief experts advise. Getting rid of a loved one's possessions after they die is one thing, but the family pictures and videos are another, and one shouldn't be too hasty in disposing of them, as I had painfully learned previously. The strategy is to pack up all your pictures in a box and wait till you're ready to face them. It may take a year or two and some may never be able to overcome the pain and sorrow brought up by looking at old pictures. There is no specific timeline to do it and everybody does it at their own pace. I was always an anxious fellow, so in my case I choose to do it as soon as possible. My theory is, if I'm in it now, why wait till later? It won't be any harder or easier, therefore let's get it over with and move on.

I have a lot more pictures than I had anticipated, as 40 years of accumulated snapshots pack up quite a few crates. I have four boxes of them actually, all filled up to the top, and the task looks daunting. But it's a beautiful day, I feel great (for a change) and confident I can take on the job, so I bring the four cartons from the basement to the veranda and get going. The first crate is easy, as it mainly contains family pictures of my youth, school friends and old family reunion shots showing smiling and laughing aunts and uncles frozen in time while eating and dancing at holiday gatherings, etc. My first attempt is a success and I pride myself at managing to have a considerable amount of fun while reminiscing, a big surprise, as I always get 'the mush' when perusing old photographs.

But the fun doesn't last long, and even if the second box starts off OK, soon melancholy sets in as the chronology of the pictures gets closer to the heart. The gorgeous face of my infant son Steve who passed away so many years ago pops up suddenly among a bunch of other photos I'm processing and immediately I feel a pinch in my chest. He was so beautiful, the image of the perfect baby smiling innocently with his big happy blue eyes looking straight at me, blond soft hair, healthy round face and pouty lips. "I miss you, buddy," I lament and, with teary eyes, I place the photo in the 'keep' file.

Many other pictures of Steve come to life through my trembling hands as I keep uncovering them out of the pile and I'm getting more and more emotional. *Geez, this is brutal*, I think. *I'll need a drink soon.* I relentlessly continue with my mission, reviewing 60 years of living, one picture at a time. I go from one remembrance to another, unsure if I should smile or cry as I get reacquainted with my past. Very few chosen ones go in the 'keep' pile and a lot in the 'burn' pile. I never look at them anyway, and when I do, I get mushy, so I may as well not have them.

After an hour of this emotionally draining task I have had enough. I fetch myself a stiff Scotch, sit comfortably by the outside wood stove and get busy sending up in smoke a huge part of a life that is no more, freeing myself of unnecessary old attachments. A hugely difficult task, but necessary if I want to become a new man. I sit there for quite a while afterwards, pondering on how difficult tomorrow will be as there are still two more crates to go. I stare at them with dread, knowing what's in them: 30 years of life with Louise. Scary...better make sure I don't run out of booze.

The third crate: my life with Louise

It's 4 p.m. and I'm sitting in the veranda, relaxing after two hours of gym and a long walk by the riverside in Lamoureux Park, ready to wrestle the infamous crates number three and four. I see them from the corner of my eye; they dare me and I hesitate a moment while I look the other way. "Brace yourself, man, you know you gotta do this. Go!" I prime myself up. "Do it. Go. Go," I repeat endlessly and, finally, reacting to my prompt, I swiftly reach for the top one and drag it between my legs in front of my adirondack chair. The bugger is heavy and I almost hurt my shoulder doing it. I untie the security latches, take a deep breath and open the Pandora's box.

With unsteady hands, I pick up one of the albums and start browsing through it. Instantly I'm transported back in time to when Louise and I met a lifetime ago, and in a flash the world around me is lost. I enter into a dimension where time and space do not exist, the past becomes present and yesterday becomes today. I go from one album to the other reviewing with melancholy dozens and dozens of snapshots highlighting the numerous trips we made together, the parties, the private intimate dinners we shared, the vacations, etc. I am mesmerized by Louise's images stilled in actions of everyday life, of us holding hands, hugging, smiling, happy, indifferent and ignorant of the difficult times ahead. And I hurt...I hurt badly.

I gulp down a respectable amount of whisky, and after my stomach calms down a bit, I go on. Sometimes laughing, sometimes crying, I breeze in a jiffy through our wedding album, barely looking at the pictures. I turn the pages quickly, not wanting to favor one picture over the other in fear of being overwhelmed by the pain. I can barely contain myself and I sob abundantly. I feel very fragile, and at some point I'm tempted to chicken out and forget the whole thing, but I go on relentlessly. This must be done, I reaffirm to myself. This is therapy, buddy. You can't spend the rest of your life being afraid of looking at a bunch of pictures and hide them in your closet; you need to desensitize yourself and make the pain disappear. Life goes on and you must go on with it, I reason to myself.

Now that the first run is over, the elimination process begins. Another sip and I go back to the first album. Doing my best to ignore the lump in my throat, I wipe the tears from my eyes with the back of my hand and I go through each photo, deciding which ones are worth keeping or burning. It is a horrendous task, but I execute it ruthlessly. The place is a mess; there are pictures thrown out half haphazardly on the porch floor. I look like a bum in my old housecoat, unshaven, disheveled hair and all, but I'm alone and I don't care. Even Max wouldn't have anything to do with me. In my case, misery doesn't like company.

Two hours later, after I'm done, the burn pile is huge while I keep just the most significant shots which I plan to insert in one single album; imagine, four crates full of pictures, the story of my life reduced into one small memorabilia portfolio, quite the job. With glass in hand, exhausted but relieved, I toast myself for a job well done, although I hope I did not eliminate too many photos; that would be regrettable. In any event, who cares really? I only need a few mementos of what things used to be; it's not good to fret excessively on the past if I want to go ahead with my new life. The best souvenirs I'll keep in my heart. More and more now, I can remember Louise with a smile and not a tear.

Without losing an instant, I grab the 'reject' boxes, carry them to the wood stove and rush to set them ablaze as fast as possible. I'm afraid that if I drag my feet on this, I'll coward up and change my mind. So, sitting in front of the outside fireplace, I feed the hungry flames as fast as I can in order to permanently obliterate the last remnants of a life that is no more. *There will be no turning back on this one*, I think, and with this final gesture, I say a final goodbye.

Time for a change, time for a new life, time for a new me, I remind myself as I watch the entrancing flames. Time to start new projects and meet new people. Giving in to a light buzz induced by the numerous shots of alcohol I've had in the previous hours, I slouch to get more comfortable, cross my legs, rest my heavy head on the high-back chair, close my eyes and lazily start cogitating on my next move.

The new me

It's eight o'clock in the morning, the sun is shining, the birds are chirping. (Sounds like the lyrics of a song, doesn't it?) I'm in a cheery disposition and I finally decide to jump out of bed. I've been awakened around six thirty this morning by the darn recycling truck which made enough bloody noise to wake up the whole neighborhood. Well, a very small neighborhood, I might say, if I consider that it consists of me, Onagh and Anna, both octogenarians who were probably hard at work already, plus a couple of annoyed dogs barking their disapproval, and a few banged-up, fur-missing, ugly-looking, fat barn cats yawning and stretching lazily, still tired from their nocturnal hunt.

In the interval, between wake and rise, I have been lying there caught up in an intriguing mix of thoughts and images bubbling up in my head like crazy. *Where's this coming from?* I ask myself, surprised at this flood of new ideas. Where I used to be brain dead, morose and down on myself most of the time, now I suddenly feel this joyful pizzazz bubbling up through every cell of my being. I feel surprisingly good and almost ready to take on the world…well, maybe not the world exactly, but something, I don't know…ahhh…hum… What do I feel like doing today? What was I saying yesterday about a 'new me,' new projects and meeting new people? Then it strikes me; the presence of life, that's what's missing.

Since Louise's passing, I had wiped out all signs of my pre-loss era as it was too painful for me to be constantly reminded of what was not anymore or never would be again. I am in a limbo, a sort of hollow static environment that needs to be perked up badly, and new pictures of the 'new me' are the answer. I will start with that and for the rest I'll be inspired later, I'm sure.

So off I go for the day; first to the local hairstylist to refresh my look (I had let my hair grow considerably in the past year), I do a bit of shopping at a few clothing stores to acquire a new accoutrement and, wearing my best jewelry, I pay a visit to the nearest portrait outlet to get a photo shoot. There you go, that'll take care of the new me. Little did I know then that creating my new identity would come only at the cost of constant efforts. But for now I'm pleased with the day and I enjoy my newfound self.

Pensively patting the soft silky hair of my faithful companion Max lying calmly by my side, I try to adopt the Zen 'sitting and doing nothing' attitude, which is in fact doing something if you really think about it. If I force myself to DO nothing, am I not in fact doing something? "Stop that, Pierre, sit and live in the moment," I scold myself. "Thinking is not Zen; you should be doing nothing, not 'thinking' about doing nothing," I remind myself one more time. Ah crap, there I go again, I'm thinking, not Zen...not Zen. Ah, forget it and have a drink. You can be Zen later.

As you can see, my abilities at achieving enlightenment suck big time and at this moment I very much prefer to give in to the kaleidoscope of exciting new thoughts and possibilities that enslave my mind. I feel good and, for a change, I look forward to what new challenges tomorrow will bring.

Creating a new website on grief, redirecting my newfound energy

In the past few months, I have been using writing as a coping mechanism and it worked very well for me, a real catharsis. It involved creating a number of articles on grief that I self-published on the internet. They related to my own experiences on loss, my pain, my sorrow and my struggle to overcome the grief caused by Louise's death. At first, the pieces were meant as a way to express my deep feelings and channel the immense build-up of negative energy I had accumulated over the years from looking after my wife as her sole caregiver. But after realizing how beneficial writing these articles was for me, I got inspired to share them with others in similar situations in the hopes that it might help them as well.

I am a member of an internet network called LinkedIn. It works pretty much the same as Facebook, except that it targets professionals looking to increase their businesses instead of being mainly a social network. I already had over 600 connec-tions, to which I sent a copy of my first article in an individual private message, asking them to forward it to anyone they knew who could benefit from it. It was an instant success, and I received dozens and dozens of testimonies from people every-where around the world telling me how they related to the article and how it helped them to cope with their own grief. It gave them hope of a better future without their loved ones.

I was ecstatic about my success, but also flabbergasted at realizing how much people needed to talk about their hurt and sorrow when they lost someone they love. Well, I sort of knew that from being in that situation myself, but it was kind of a shock to hear it straight from the horse's mouth. What struck me the most though was the lack of support available for grieving people living in remote areas, or even large cities in less fortunate countries. Even in many Canadian provinces and American states, grief support centers are not readily available.

I have benefited greatly from the help the 'Bereaved Families of Ontario' (BFO) brought me in my darkest moments, and I naively thought that everyone in need could be as blessed as I was. But that was not the case at all. For instance, the neighboring province of Quebec doesn't have services for grievers that even come close to those of the BFO. That seems so unfortunate to me, so I decide I must do something about this and I sit down for a brainstorming session. It doesn't take me long to come up with an answer: a free online support group on the LinkedIn network.

In a jiffy, I set up the group and name it: 'Share your pain— grieving successfully.' The idea is simple: open a free LinkedIn account, navigate to the group section, search for 'share your pain - grieving successfully' and request to join the group. Once the request is accepted, members can start a discussion on a grief theme, share their story, their pain, their sorrow, ask questions, seek advice, or respond to another member's story. In other words, isolation doesn't exist anymore, and whatever remote area in the world a needy soul may reside, they still can be part of a caring and non-judgmental community that shares similar interests. People can talk freely and express their profound and personal feelings with complete anonymity if it's what they wish.

Once all the details are in place and the group is functional, I immediately send a notice to all my LinkedIn connections asking them to either join themselves or relay the invitation to anybody they know who is in need of such a service. The response is immediate and the membership requests start rolling in. People get involved in new discussions, participate in conversations about their feelings of loss, and it's an absolute beauty to see them exchanging like this. I feel proud to have created such an efficient needed outlet and a voice for those who would otherwise have had to remain silent. My new baby, let's see how far it goes.

Are my reactions determined by fate, karma or coincidence? Are my actions meant to be part of a predestined karmic plan or am I just an opportunist learning to adapt in a strange random world? Who knows? I'm not brainy enough to answer that one. One thing is for sure, if Louise would not have died, all these wonderful occurrences would not have existed and I would not be the man I am today. In view of this, isn't the concept of good and bad just a matter of perspective? Life does not point the finger, judge, punish or reward; it just is, and nothing should be expected from it.

Encouraged by the success of my online grieving group, I want to do more to help and I decide to create a website on grieving. Guess what its name is? www.shareyourpain-grieving-successfully.com and its mission is basically the same as my online support group. People can still contact me directly through the site, but it's mainly an informative tool on grieving where visitors can view videos, hear music, read articles, and get book suggestions and addresses for other grieving websites and support groups. It is a great place to hang out for a grieving person, and I'm proud to be able to bring in my modest contribution in helping my brothers and sisters rebuild their lives after their devastating loss.

Chapter 10

Pre-Loss:
December 14 2009
The beginning of the end
Depression, anger, bargaining, hope, despair

I can't remember what the movie was all about, for I kept bringing my attention to Louise who was constantly grabbing her head with both hands in an effort to ease the headache that was plaguing her. She did not make much of it though, and asked me to try not to worry and enjoy the movie. But deep inside, I was troubled and wondered if the weird incidents that had occurred recently had anything to do with her headache.

Strange unexplained things had been happening to Louise in the last few months even though she was feeling better all around. For instance, one time as she was processing an invoice for a customer, as hard as she tried to write the number four, the number seven would always come out. Other times she could not add up a series of numbers properly, which was out of character for a mathematical ace like she was. Occasionally, her eye–hand coordination was completely off. For instance, she would awkwardly miss touching something within her reach.

But the headache was a new one, which was surprising as she was doing so well recently. So well in fact that she had even contemplated going back to work in the New Year. The result of her last scan showed no traces of cancer left in her abdomen, her energy was up to normal and she felt good all around. Intrigued and suspicious, I wondered what was going on.

When the movie ended and as we were walking out towards the exit, Louise had a strange air about her. She looked as if she was in a daze and out of it. Suddenly, as I opened the door for her to walk out, she rapidly and for absolutely no reason at all made a sharp left turn and walked forcefully into a large concrete pillar, banging her head violently. The force of the impact was so strong it almost knocked her out and I had to reach and hold her so she would not fall onto the sidewalk. At that moment, holding her head tightly with both hands, she kept blinking her eyes rapidly, moaning in pain.

Thankfully, the pain eased up progressively and had disappeared by the time we arrived home, which was a good thing as the prospect of spending hours vegging in the hospital's waiting room did not appeal to me at all, I mean 'not at all'.

But the minute we set foot in the house I immediately called our family doctor who agreed to see Louise on the spot. From then on, everything went at lightning speed. After a quick examination, and suspecting the worst, Dr E. used his influence to arrange a consultation with a neurologist friend of his and, in turn, the neurologist pressured the hospital for an emergency brain scan. The scan was performed in a flash and off we were on our way back to the neurologist's office to learn of the results.

Everything went so fast, we barely had time to think about what was happening. But I had an ugly gut feeling, an awful sense of dread that our life was about to turn to shit again. Sitting in the neurologist's waiting room I felt very jittery and scared stiff about learning the truth. We did not have to wait long, and as soon as we sat in those two little ridiculous spartan chairs facing the doc's desk, he let us have it without preamble. "Mrs Milot, you have two large cancerous tumors lodged in very sensitive areas of the brain and they are too encroached in surrounding tissue to even consider surgery. Your only option left is radiotherapy." After Louise gave her consent, he immediately made arrangements with the Ottawa Cancer Centre to start treatments as soon as possible. He also prescribed an anticonvulsion medication and Dexamethasone, a corticosteroid meant to reduce inflammation around the tumors and thus bring some relief to Louise until the end of the zapping treatments.

We could not even fathom that the very medication meant to help make Louise's life more bearable would soon become one of the most important factors in her demise. Thus began my hardest struggle yet. I should talk in terms of 'we' here, but it seems that from that period on and to the end of Louise's life, I became the pillar of this devastating unwanted journey. Was her apparent indifference due to the tumors, a lack of ability in taking in the full impact of the situation, or that she was starting to give up? I really couldn't tell, but I felt alone and crushed under an enormous weight. I sensed more than ever that a good part of Louise's recovery depended on me and I wondered despairingly how I could manage to hold on through this new onslaught.

I was tired and discouraged from the years of fighting the never-ending roller-coaster ride of hope and dread. I was losing weight at an alarming rate as I barely ate, and I was terrified at the thought that I could become sick myself. I was often dizzy and plagued by a persistent dry cough, a painful earache and a lump in my throat the size a of small golf ball that would not go away, reminding me that I could also have cancer. I had heart palpitations and my blood pressure was shooting through the roof. I suspected that a lot of other things were wrong with me, including a messed-up mind, but I chose to ignore them; there was no time for this.

Why I elected not to request help from the health services I don't know. Although I could have had a volunteer to look after Louise while I rested, went to see a movie, or to shop or do something else to allow me a much-needed change of scenery, I stubbornly rejected any offer of support. Was stupid male ego or need for control at play in this scenario? I think not. I suspect that the main reason why I behaved this way is that I did not trust anyone or believe that anybody could look after Louise as well as I could. She was my responsibility, 'for better or for worse.' I swore that promise once and I would stand up to the task till the end, whatever the cost might be. I am a protector, always have been; it's in my nature and I can't help it.

My first order of business in dealing with the administration of the drug was to work with the pharmacist in order to find a brand of medication that was lactose-free, as Louise was intolerant to this substance. Not easy, as most medication in pill form contains lactose and the only brand that did not had to be specially ordered. Little did I know then that that insignificant detail would become an increasing source of aggravation for me over the months. Eventually Pat, my pharmacist, a dear for her precious help, patience and understanding, found a lactose-free brand and placed the order which would take three to four days for delivery. But meanwhile she provided Louise with a short supply of meds to support her while the right brand arrived. Louise's condition was too precarious to run the risk of going into convulsions.

It wasn't long before we got a call from the Cancer Centre and Louise's first radiotherapy session was booked. Before though, she had to meet with the onco-radiologist to evaluate and formulate the right kind of treatment for her. Dr L., a short man with a gentle face and mild manners, walked into the room with the confidence that doctors often display (easy when you're on the other side of the fence), read Louise's file for a short while and then walked directly towards her, took her hand reassuringly, sat down on a stool in front of her, with kind but intent eyes looked straight at her, and asked intriguingly, "Mrs Milot, do you know what's happening to you?"

I have been hit many times in my life, physically, intellectually, emotionally and spiritually, and I have learned that often the hardest blows do not always come from the most evident sources. The doctor's question was a rhetorical one if I ever heard one and it hit me like a bomb. I could tell right there and then that he was an expert at his job, not only in the field of treating cancer, but also at announcing succinctly to patients that their chances of survival from a disease amounted to zilch, zero, *kaput*, *finis*, you're dead!

Louise did not seem to catch the innuendo; she was too fazed out. I did get the message though, loud and clear. That short loaded sentence shook me to the core and swiftly pulled the rug from under my feet. From that moment on, something clicked in me and I became an automaton; doing my care provider job as best as I knew how, while burying my joys, fears, hopes and hanging on as passively as I could for the inevitable.

If the doctor's behavior was subtle and reserved in the beginning of the consultation, he could not have been more direct and to the point after examining Louise and perusing her brain scan results in greater detail. "Mrs Milot, I can't tell you if the treatments will prolong your life for a month or two or even that you will be able to celebrate next Christmas with your family, but I would start talking to my loved ones about the seriousness of my condition if I were you." Wham! There you go! What a nice way to put it. Congrats, Doc. Then again in all honesty, what other choice did he have? How else could he tell Louise that her hours were counted? Not easy. What a depressing job his must be.

In my mind, I understood that, but it just hurt to learn the truth and accept the devastating reality that Louise was slipping through my fingers...again. That I was losing the one person that meant everything to me. At that point I was pretty certain that my life was about to become a horrendous hell-ride with crushing loneliness and despair. My fear factor scale had just climbed up a couple of notches.

I couldn't help asking myself haunting questions: What the hell are we doing all this for then? Why go on with this charade if it's going to turn to crap anyway? What's the point? Why? Why? Why? Like all the other times before, my conclusion was that when backed up to the wall and facing the obligation of making life or death decisions, we grasp at straws and hope for miracles. What if it would work this time?

Again we choose to fight because it's ingrained in our being; it's survival instinct; it's because we cannot accept defeat without a fight, as hopeless as it may seem; we have to do it, it's human nature. We fight because we are not mature and wise enough to determine when the time is up, especially when it comes to making the decision for someone else who can't do it for themselves anymore. How do we announce to a sick loved one that we don't have faith in them anymore, that we think that they can't beat this thing and that they should lie down and die? What right do we have to make this kind of decision? Simple. We don't. At least I didn't and I tried my very best to accept the fact that Louise had her own reasons to battle, her own timeline; it was her indisputable right and I could only stand by supportively, even if it killed me. Doing something is better than doing nothing, we concluded, and decided to go ahead with the treatment and ignore the doctor's comment.

The treatment sessions were surprisingly brief; five sessions of five minutes each per week and it was a 'complete brain sweep.' The sessions took place at the Ottawa Civic Centre hospital, a revamped building in the crowded east part of Ottawa. Parking the car was a dubious task as there never seemed to be enough parking spaces in the main covered lot, which forced us to drop off our vehicle in one of the surrounding streets and drag our asses up a slippery windy little freaking slope back to the main entrance of the hospital.

Climbing that hill against the wind was always an exhausting endeavor for Louise as her legs had become very weak over the two years of fighting the battle. It pained me to see her huff and puff as she was bravely making her way back to the building all bundled up in her long black heavy winter coat. What a gal. Even with my help she could barely make it. Dropping her off at the entrance was also not an option: no sitting space or wheelchairs available, and leaving her alone standing up while I was gone to park the car was risky at best.

The first visit was spent by having a mask of Louise's face and head made. It was meant to hold her head steady during the irradiation sessions. The mask was hideous and scary enough to act as a prop in a *Friday the 13th* movie. It was terrifying mainly for what it represented: morbidity and dreadfulness. After the sessions were over, the mask was given back to Louise and she would occasionally use it as a joke to scare people off at parties. After she passed, I found the horrible gizmo at the bottom of a box buried in the basement and it looked as horrifying as ever. I threw it away immediately.

Except for the fact that the long walk from the entrance of the hospital to the irradiation room in the basement was a major effort for Louise, everything went well. There was virtually no wait time before each of the sessions which were brief as promised. 'Zip zap' and she was out of there as if nothing had happened. Anyone looking at her could not tell that she had just had her brain fried. On our way back home, while I was driving, I would discreetly spy on Louise to try and detect any signs that she could be freaking out or falling into convulsions. Nothing. She looked completely normal. Reassuring for the moment, but what good can come out of this? What could the consequences be in the near future? Recovery? Cure? Surely not, as the doctor definitely took that possibility away, but maybe stabilization would be a good compromise for the moment. After that, who knows? Your guess is as good as mine. It could go either way; she could be healed miraculously by the intervention of the Divine Spirit (yeah right)! And not go 'gaga' from the zapping, or she could still be strolling along *en route* to decrepitude while the tumors kept eating at her. This would remain to be seen. I was nervous and on the look-out for any signs of disturbances that could indicate trouble. So far so good, I thought.

This scenario repeated itself for five more weeks until it was time for another brain scan to determine the state of the rent-free guests in Louise's skull. Of course, there was a time interval necessary to allow radiation to do its job and hopefully vaporize the big bad guys in her head. Until that time arrived, the wait consisted of worried thoughts, hope, fears, bargaining, anger and freaking pills. What a pain in the neck that was, more for me than for Louise I should say. She was understandably passive and a little out of it most of the time, so as her sole caretaker, I had to be proactive.

I had to work up and update complicated schedules regularly; it was horrendous and it weighed heavily on me. You have to understand that I am an artist and I have an aversion to everything which is closely related to numbers, charts, spread-sheets or additions...well, except for the money in my bank account. So, on top of cooking, washing, cleaning and doing all the darn shebang a housewife has to do, my days consisted of loading up on caffeine to fire up my tired brain cells and concoct some kind of workable schedule for Louise's meds. It was hell on earth to try and figure it out.

You see, according to medical documentation, corticosteroids and anti-convulsive medication don't work very well together and the possible side effects from the negative interactions between the two drugs were always a concern. Thus, the need to wean out the anti-convulsive med as soon as possible was a must and I would have to get my butt moving on this one and presto. Louise never had convulsions and it wasn't clear if the drug was really needed. Louise came to my rescue on that one though, as in a moment of strength and clarity she made an executive decision and, in spite of the doctor's advice, decided to get off the med 'cold turkey.' "To hell with this, it makes me feel weird all the time and I'm tired of it," she said. "Screw it, this junk is taking a hike. I'll chance it." And so that was that for that pill; one less headache for me but a dozen notches more on my stress-level ladder.

It never ends; this is a 'no win' situation. I felt caught between a rock and a hard spot. Now I'll have to follow her like a needy puppy to make sure she doesn't go into a fit at the top of the stairs, roll down rattling and shaking, and break her neck. Gawd, it's an awful way of putting it, I know, but it was true. In all honesty I have to admit that over time an underlying sense of resentment was growing inside of me like a huge shameful dark cloud. I felt guilty; boy, did I ever. What a miserable position to be in for a caregiver: battling conflicting emotions of love, anger and fear in an arena of despair and helplessness while at the same time remaining detached and efficient. What I would not have given to be able to walk away from it all, grab Louise by the hand and run and run into oblivion. My resentment was not aimed at Louise of course; the poor soul was just trying her best to survive in this fuzzy ocean of confusion. But I was pissed at the whole freaking mess I was thrown into.

Even though I was rid of the anti-convulsing drug, I still had the task of managing the administration of the corticosteroid drug and it was a doozy. You see, Brand X, the kind that Louise was taking, comes in the form of a small yellow pill and, make no mistake about it, the tablet may seem harmless just by looking at it, but the little overzealous bugger is extremely powerful and plays its role with great enthusiasm. In the end, the efficacy of this so-called miracle med will become one of the most important factors in Louise's demise and my worse source of stress.

You see, our bodies react this way: when a body part is injured or diseased, our body reacts by creating a build-up of fluid in the affected area. Inflammation or swelling is created by the organism as an attempt at self-protection, the aim being to remove harmful stimuli, damaged cells, irritants or pathogens and to allow the body to begin the healing process. But sometimes under extraordinary conditions or when the injury is too overwhelming, the body will overreact and produce massive edemas capable of creating havoc when it compresses tissues surrounding the diseased area, as it did around Louise's brain tumor. When that unfortunate situation occurs, the swelling then needs to be controlled rapidly with medication. That's when our little buddy comes into play and starts doing what it's supposed to do: boost the adrenal gland's capabilities of secreting anti-inflammatory hormone. In fact, in most cases our eager little friend more than supports the adrenal glands; it literally takes over for the overwhelmed and tired glands while the healing process takes place. And that, ladies and gentlemen, was the source of our problems as we will see later.

The scenario on paper looks very cute, simple and wonderful as in all fairy tales, but there is a 'bump in the road' as the notorious French Inspector Clouseau would say. Aside from its devastating side effects (making the bones dramatically more brittle, among other horrors), the med is very highly addictive and that's why Louise could not stay on it for an extended period of time. Six weeks maximum with an adequate weaning period was the norm. Thus, our good Dr L. recommended that Louise stay on the drug for the duration of the treatments and worked out a weaning schedule that should start immediately after the last irradiation session.

Imagine that, six weeks tops on the drug and Louise stayed on it until she died ten months later. No wonder she was in such a discombobulated state when she rang her last bell. Well, I guess we're all in some sort of a horrible mess when we cross the Pearly Gate to meet our maker. That's why we die, right? But some leave this Earth in a less graceful manner than others, and poor Louise was in such a miserable state that if it would not have hurt me so much to lose her, I would almost have been happy to see her go sooner. Still hurts to think about it.

Why do some lucky bastards shut their lights off with a beaming smile on their faces as if they just had the best sex of their lives and other unfortunate dudes cross over in excruci-ating pain, begging for a compassionate hand to end their misery? A big mystery, and don't drool on me crap like 'God works in mysterious ways,' or 'pain is the best teacher,' blah,

blah, blah. I think it's BS and it would only infuriate me further. Well, for now at least, and I may change my mind should the 'Big Guy' decide to strike me down with a slap in the back of the head to prove this hogwash is all true. Naah! Really. I don't think so. Anyway, I truly think that no earthling is enlightened enough to answer that brain twister yet, certainly not me.

But enough with the spiritual cogitation and let's hitch a ride back on our train to disaster. Administering the drug to Louise in increasing doses as the doctor prescribed was easy enough and during that time Louise was stable at all levels.

The problems only started towards the end of the weaning-out phase. Each time we were close to eliminating the stupid drug, Louise started to freak out and we had to re-increase the dosage progressively until she was stabilized again. What a yo-yo ride that was.

When she was stabilized, she became her old self again, well almost; she could master high levels of Sudoku puzzles easily, knit intricate patterns like an expert, carry on intelligent and sophisticated conversations, and so on. During those periods, I felt I was home again. I felt she was back with me, we were a functional couple once more…well, for a little while at least, and even though I still carried some feeble hope that she could recover, I knew the good time wouldn't last. I could almost read the writing on the wall and I knew it was just a matter of how long. What an emotional struggle it has been.

Had I listened to my inner voice warning me of the outcome and not been so stubborn in my quest for healing, we could have avoided so many hardships and could have embraced life to the fullest for the very little time that Louise had left. But we couldn't be sure, we couldn't know how long she had and, as I said before, our instinct is to fight, and fight we did, in every way possible. Up and down and up and down we went on the damn roller-coaster ride. As high as I would get when she was on top, as low, desperate, hurt and angry I became when I helplessly witnessed her plunging progressively back into darkness when the drug lost its effectiveness due to the weaning.

The Sudoku puzzles were always the first to go as she went from solving expert levels to not even being able to remember how to solve the beginner ones. I am reminded of this every time I look at the ink pen marks left on my yellow bedsheets where her place used to be. One particular night she was so out of it that she wrote on the sheet instead of in her game book. I felt so sorry for her. How could I not? Louise, such a bright and intelligent girl, reduced to this. This hurts so bad I can barely stand it and I'm typing like a blind man because my wet eyes can barely read the computer screen.

The brain is a bizarre beast with wide unknown territories and I was subject to that fact almost every day at mealtime with Louise's weird behavior with the kitchen utensils. For instance, as hard as she tried, she could not hold her fork the right side up, with the frustrating result that her food was always falling off of it before it reached her mouth. The same thing happened with her cutting knife and, no matter how hard she tried, she would always end up holding it with the sharp edge up as she would desperately and unsuccessfully try to cut her food. At other times, if she by any chance did succeed in forking a piece of meat, she could rarely make it reach its destination but instead ended up shoving it everywhere else in her face but in her mouth. At some point, I had to steady her hand and feed her like an inexperienced baby. I think at this point it is futile to elaborate on my exasperation (hers also, I'm sure) at watching her try to operate more complicated instruments such as the telephone or the television remote control. I think you get the idea.

What drove me crazy about that drug is that it took as long to kick in as it took to wean out. It was exasperating and so discouraging. Up until the end of the weaning phase, Louise was stable and we thought that we had it all under control. We could see the light at the end of the tunnel and carried out hopes of getting rid of that darn drug for good. But all of a sudden, wham, here we went again. Within a day, Louise would start to have that distant look in her eyes, forks and knives would start taking a life of their own, and her ability to do Sudoku puzzles, well... Everything was going downhill and turning to shit again. I was devastated each time that scenario occurred, as I knew very well that we would have to start all over one more time. It also meant that Louise was not making any progress. It would take at least another two to three weeks for Louise to become stabilized and functional once more as the drug had to be re-introduced progressively. Even if I would have maxed out the drug on Louise, it would not have made a damn difference. Corticosteroid drugs are particular this way.

The situation was further complicated when we experimented with substituting the chemical drug with a natural anti-inflammatory medication. Whoa, wrong move. Brand X did not like this at all and threatened to shut down operations totally. The introduction of curcumin, or any other natural anti-inflammatory medication for that matter, interfered and reduced dramatically the efficiency of the chemical one. No matter how many times we tried, each attempt was plagued with the same result: disaster. So, reluctantly, we had to let that go and stick with the chemicals. Damn. Louise's situation was too precarious to fool around with in unknown territory.

In retrospect, I think that Louise's adrenal glands must have already been diseased, collapsed or too tired to kick back into action when Brand X was no longer active in her system. Patients taking that drug often experience similar results as their adrenal glands become lazy and reluctant to go back to work once more. In Louise's case though, I suspect that it was more than that. Her kidneys and adrenals must have been completely exhausted, either by fighting the cancer or by the constant effort they made to eliminate the massive amount of crappy chemicals pumped into her veins over the years.

This 'climb and slide' ride went on for months and consumed all of our time and energy. Winter became spring, spring became summer and Louise kept on declining progressively. Her body and face had swollen up so much under the influence of the drug's side effects ('moon face' is the term for this) that I had to buy her extra-large pajamas which was the only clothing she could wear. Her ankles were inflamed to the point that she could only wear diabetics' socks, and even then, they would still cut the blood flow in her feet and leave a serious indentation on her ankles. Her tummy was so swollen, she looked like a nine-months pregnant woman, and her face was round, red and puffy.

Towards the end of the summer, she could barely stand up and walk by herself. I had to install security handles so she could grab onto them as she wobbled miserably from the bedroom to the bathroom. Even then I had to assist her most of the time. Sitting on the adapted toilet seat became quite an ordeal for her, and for me I have to say, as I often had to redirect her butt to the seat or squarely pick her up from the ground when she missed the target. She had become a heavy person because of all the swelling and water retention and it was a real workout for me to hoist her limp body up again. With no strength in her legs, it was extremely difficult for her to stand up out of that contraption, and from time to time she would tip forward, dangerously menacing to fall face first into the bathtub facing the toilet seat, and I had to steady her so that didn't happen.

I will not go into more details, out of respect and dignity here, but I will just mention that my task as a caregiver did not end there, and at that point I had to take over all of her personal care, hygiene and toiletries, including washing her, combing her hair, brushing her teeth and dressing her, cooking her meals and helping her eat. I really didn't mind at that point. I had become an automaton and I was doing what needed to be done, no questions asked.

Everything was kind of OK this way, but of course the

situation took another turn downward when she could no longer walk down the stairs without falling. Her legs were too weak and would give out without warning; she would fall on her butt and I had to help her get down the remaining steps. I got into the habit of walking down the stairs before her while she would hang on to me by the shoulders, neck, head or anywhere else she could grab on to me in order not to tumble down.

We managed like this for a while until one day it was not enough and she crumbled on the stairs behind me, making an awful unhealthy muffled sound, like bones connecting brutally with a carpeted hard surface. *This will leave bad marks and bruises,* I thought and was the motivation I needed to resign myself to setting up her living quarters downstairs in the living room from now on. It would be safer this way, I thought. As a result of this decision, the little guy inside my head was starting to whisper a message I was reluctant to hear, and with sadness I concluded that the parlor would become her last place of residence. At that moment, a fissure broke through my carapace and I was overwhelmed by a massive wave of despair at the approaching end.

Chapter 11

Pre-Loss:
September 2010
Can one ever die in dignity?
Fear, resentment, sadness, feeling of uselessness and final
acceptance

Can any adult ever consider having to go through the embarrassment of wearing diapers? I'm sure that that thought at some point has crossed everyone's mind. "I would never do that," some would say with gusto and reject the idea with a wave of the hand. "I'd rather die than be humiliated this way." Louise and I used to make light fun of that possibility as we would watch senior diapers television commercials. "Can you picture yourself walking around with your butt wrapped up in this ridiculous accoutrement?" I would jokingly ask. "How sexy would that be? How tight and uncomfortable would you be with this lump of material tucked up in your denim pants?" And on and on we would go. We knew of course that it could be a curse for those plagued with having to wear the darn thing, but the jokes were all done without sarcasm and in good clean fun.

Over the years, this cute little farce went on and we never even opened the door to the possibility that it could really happen to either one of us. Life has a wicked sense of humor sometimes and can unexpectedly throw nasty curves at us, as we had painfully found out some time before.

It was a nice bright sunny day and Louise and I were driving lazily on the road bordering the St Lawrence River around the cozy little community of Summerstown. The view was gorgeous and the air smelled of wild flowers and decaying grass on the waterside. It was a typical summer day, the kind you wish for on a cold wintry morning. But I could not really enjoy it as Louise was growing restless and was rapidly showing signs of fatigue, which was raising a red flag in my mind. I feared that we would have to shorten our little voyage and go back home in haste.

That Monday afternoon, Louise, feeling on an upswing, suddenly perked up and wanted to go out for a drive. It was rare that this happened now and so, taking advantage of her little spurt of energy, I geared up and prepared her for the outing without a second thought. *Que sera sera...* If dressing her was an experience in itself, getting her to the car was quite an adventure, but I succeeded anyway and off we were to see the wizard. Louise was happy and that's all that counted for now.

As I feared, the fun didn't last long and soon enough we had to rush back home. Louise had to 'go' and it was urgent, no fooling around with that. I had learned my lesson the hard way a few times before. Even the lightning trip back to the house didn't cut it, and as soon as we crossed the entrance door she couldn't hold it anymore and to her greatest embarrassment made a mess of herself. From now on, it would be diapers whether she liked it or not, I thought, a little irritated. She had been resisting the idea for a while, but I decided that this last episode did it. So, after cleaning up like a good boy, I sat her comfortably in our leather couch, tuned the television on to her favorite show and rushed back out to the drug store to pick up the 'item.'

It was one of those super drugstores with never-ending aisles, but nevertheless it did not take me long to locate the adult diaper section. One cannot imagine how many brands, sizes, types or colors are available. How many people wear these things...? Hum, I wondered if I knew some of them. After many deliberations and calculations I finally made up my mind on what I hoped was the right choice and walked swiftly to the cash register to pay for my purchase. As I deposited my not-so-discreet diaper package on the counter, I felt as if a hundred eyes were staring at me, sizing up my butt to figure out if I was wearing one. I felt flushed and uncomfortable like the first time I bought sanitary napkins for my ex-wife or acquired my first condom. Get a grip of yourself, buddy. Better get used to this reality and make nothing of it; this is your life from now on, man, and I wasn't laughing anymore.

Saying that the diapers made my life easier would be a gross exaggeration. I had no more mess to clean up, but now I had diapers to change. It was a winning trade-off though, but the embarrassment for Louise was still there, especially in her moments of clarity which now occurred less and less often. The drugs and cancer were taking their toll.

Since she could no longer climb the stairs to go to the bathroom, I had to install a commode by the side of the couch where she lay now most of the time, watching television or sleeping. Poor soul, what else could she do? Sudoku puzzles, knitting, crosswords, typing and reading were all things of the past. Heck, she couldn't even turn on the TV by herself or dial the telephone. All these tasks and gizmos (TV remote and wireless telephone) had become alien to her and a constant source of frustration every time she stubbornly tried to figure them out.

I set the commode as close to the divan as I could so that Louise would just have to switch from one place to the other, thus minimizing the risk of falling. That worked well for a while, even though I had to keep an eye on her, constantly ready to assist her. Try to imagine how embarrassed you would feel doing your 'thing' right in the middle of the living room while someone is watching you. I gave her space at first of course, closed the curtains I had set up for privacy and kept my looks discreet, but eventually I had to intervene as the motion of getting up, sitting down, getting up and sitting down again became too much for her. At that point, I had to help her out with the whole shebang, including personal hygiene which understandably added another notch to her uneasiness.

Although she never told me in so many words, I knew by the look on her face that she felt awful and guilty to watch me, numerous times a day, grab the commode's detachable container, run up the stairs to ditch its contents in the toilet, clean it, come back downstairs and get things ready for another run.

In view of all this, when you think about it seriously, in the end, losing one's sense of reality is a blessing and most certainly lessens the emotional pain for those going down the final slide.

I so wish I don't have to go through this crap (literally) when my time comes. Let me die struck by a lightning bolt, a speeding truck, a falling tree, suffer a heart attack while having sex or, better yet, slip out smoothly while sleeping in a comfy bed. Anything is better than suffering the pain and indignities that Louise went through. But then again, life may have other plans for me; I just have to hope for the best. Maybe this life thing is just a big game of heads or tails where the flavor of our fate depends on which side the coin falls. In times of confusion like this though, I force myself to draw from my Zen teaching to find solace by the re-affirmation that nothing else in life counts but the present moment, like for instance, sipping a delicious single-malt Scotch while playing at being a writer!

Things got even more complicated when the inflammation got worse. Her feet, ankles and calves were swollen to the point that she could no longer wear socks or slippers. To alleviate that, her legs had to be elevated most of the time. Our leather couch was one of those L-shaped sectionals with two lazy-boys at each end. I had to tuck up Louise in the one closest to the commode, inclining the chair so that her legs would be supported as high as possible. Even that was not enough and I had to raise them further by stuffing a huge cushion under her feet that I kept wrapped up in a blanket to keep them warm. This and the diuretic pills that were prescribed by her doctor seemed to work fine…for now.

Needless to say, in her condition, getting out of that contraption was quite a challenge for her and, even with my help, she managed to make a few falls serious enough to leave a few nasty bruises.

To my greatest dismay (and hers too, I'm sure), her breathing had become progressively laborious and she would mispronounce a word here and there. It drove me crazy to listen and watch her try to carry on a conversation as she was constantly gasping for air. At first, the gasps were very subtle and barely noticeable, but over time they became pretty obvious and I could not, for the love of life, refrain from trying to breathe for her to compensate. I suspected of course that something was wrong and I was torn between wanting to know the truth and the unrealistic hope that this would disappear miraculously. I didn't know yet, but unfortunately, the truth was about to come out…soon.

October 2010

The day the real pain started

It was just another day and we seemed to have fallen into some kind of routine with the back and forth from the couch to the commode. I was always standing by very close now, ready to assist her with the motion, and Louise didn't seem to mind so much anymore. Like she did so many times before, as she was sitting on the commode, shakily she lifted herself off the bench slightly, bent forward and was struggling to grab her pajama bottom in an effort to lift it back up to her waist when, all of a sudden, I heard her make a sudden faint muffled scream and her face contorted into a painful grimace as she heavily fell back down on the seat in agony; she had just fractured a vertebra. Her bones had become so brittle as a result of taking the corticosteroid long term, it was all it took to break her back. Damn pills! But we didn't know that yet, or even suspect it was close to that, even when Louise insisted that she had heard a crack in the middle of her back.

If I thought it was difficult to move her from one position to another, I hadn't seen anything yet. Getting her out of her precarious position on the bench, cleaning her, dressing her and dragging her back onto the couch was an absolute horror. With all the swelling, the water retention and the extra fat she had accumulated over the months from the drugs, her body weight had increased tremendously. She must have pushed the scale up to at least 180 pounds and, with no strength in her legs and arms, she had become a considerable dead weight to move around. With great effort and a half-broken back (mine this time) I finally managed to drop her onto the couch where she somehow wiggled herself into a comfortable position...and stopped screaming. Sitting this way, the pain was lessened considerably and, as long as she didn't move too much, it was tolerable.

My state of mind at this time was difficult to describe. It was a mixed bag of panic, fear, panic, anger, panic, and panic again. I felt helpless...again, and when anger left me for a few minutes, panic would set back in with a vengeance. I had lost all my composure and emotional numbness and I was pacing like a caged lion. My face was flushed and I had the shakes. In a mixture of talking/screaming, I kept repeating to no one in particular: "I'm taking you to the hospital, right now, this instant, let's go." But Louise wouldn't have it; she would not, could not move and was staying there helplessly like a wounded animal. She was too exhausted to even consider getting out of that couch, which added to my desperation.

Finally, after some time had passed, I realized that my little outburst was getting me nowhere and was creating more harm than good to both of us. I got a grip on myself and finally calmed down. But it was too late, the damage had been done, and when I dared to look at Louise again, my heart sank as I saw her frightened desperate look and the tears rolling down her face. "I'm sorry, I'm so sorry I raised my voice, honey," I lamented and rushed to get the bottle of painkillers. She had been taking them for a while now to ease the pain of the multiple bumps and bruises from falling all over the place. Previously the pain was minor, nothing compared to this. I doubted very much they could do the job this time. After giving her two extra-strength tablets, I called the hospital to inquire as to what I should do. The attending nurse recommended that since the pain had subsided, it could only be a bad strain and that it might go away by itself in a few days. "In the meantime give her two 500 milligrams of acetaminophen every four hours, and if the situation reoccurs tomorrow, bring her immediately to the emergency room." Somehow, talking to a medical attendant helped my stress level go down a few notches, but still, I remained doubtful, fidgety and overly alert. I had this gut feeling that something was very different this time and that the night would be long, excruciatingly long.

As I sat there staring into dead space, I was cogitating on how the hell I would manage to bring her to the hospital in that condition if it came to that. The car would not do, that's for sure. I would most certainly need an ambulance, so I had better get ready. *Well, we're not there yet; let's wait and see for now,* I decided. Unbeknown to me, though, the wait would not be long, as I was about to find out.

All the while she was buried comfortably in the 'Lazy-Boy' chair with her legs raised and extended in front of her, her condition was stable and fairly pain-free. But of course, she could not remain motionless forever, and all the devils from hell would resurface to stab, poke and pierce her beaten back with excruciating pain every time she tried to change position or lie down on her side to sleep. Transporting her to the commode to relieve herself was a harrowing experience and I'm afraid I'll still be haunted by the sounds of her horrible screams and moans until the day I die.

As I said before, I expected the night to be long, and it was. It was endless, the longest I had ever known, and by morning I had made an executive decision: Louise was checking into the hospital, period. No ifs, ands or buts.

After the medics arrived and saw her in that condition, they did not lose an instant and rushed her to the Cornwall Community Hospital for immediate care. At that moment, I felt guilty for not having taken that decision earlier into the night. I should have argued more with Louise to persuade her to change her mind about the hospital, but she was a stubborn woman and did not let go easily. It was finished now though; I had to get over my emotions and go forward, but forward to what? I asked myself. It didn't take long for the answer to come and it appeared more as a feeling than anything else. Intuitively I knew that we were embarking on a downhill slide from which there was no coming back up. My heart made a double beat and I entered the ambulance with a stabbing pain in my gut, getting ready for the worst.

If I thought that the preceding night was long and emotionally draining, I hadn't seen anything yet, as the four-day wait in the emergency room was brutal and beyond exhausting. With nothing else to sit on but the single straight chair available in the room, my back was a wreck and, towards the end, was screaming to the almighty every time I moved. The food, well, what can I say about the food. Aside from the fact that it was tasteless and inedible, it was a definite no-no for me. I suffer from all kinds of food allergies and intolerances and if I had eaten even one bite of the slush they were serving, I would have been on my back and rendered useless for days. This situation was unacceptable of course. I was Louise's backup and I had to stay strong for her. Not that the food was all that terrible really, but like most industrially processed grub, it contained all kinds of modified dairy ingredients and other chemicals that my temperamental digestive system cannot tolerate.

I subsisted mainly on peanuts, chips, coke and an occasional hamburger. I was not very hungry anyhow and food had little appeal to me. Being in that jungle of moans and groans, patched-up body parts, broken arms and legs and wincing faces was getting to me in an indescribable way. The beeps and bleeps of the medical equipment, the multitude of tubes hooked up to needles stuck deep into arms and hands of patients, and the constant enervating buzz of the emergency room gave me the creeps and turned my stomach upside down.

But my distress was mainly caused by the person in ER21. Louise had been lying in that room for days now being poked, pierced, drained, X-rayed, pumped full of fluids...and still her condition had not improved. In fact, by the looks of the attending doctors, the situation looked bleak. Often I would have to leave the room, either because I was not allowed to witness a certain risky procedure or because I could downright not stand the sight of a medieval-looking instrument of torture, such as long menacing needles piercing Louise's lungs to drain the fluid in there.

Poor baby, how I ached for her and how I wished I could end all this crap and take her home with me. Little did I know then that my wish would come true sooner than expected, but not in the way I was hoping for.

We were on the fourth day of Louise's never-ending stay in the emergency room when I saw Dr G. walking towards me with a blank look on his young face. He had light red hair and a pale freckled complexion reminiscent of Irish people. He looked thin in his reddish-brown uniform and was strolling along calmly and purposefully holding a clear flask of liquid in his right hand. He had just drained Louise's lung and was coming to give me the results of the analysis they had made of the extracted fluid. My heart took a double beat.

I guess when one deals with this kind of stuff day in and day out, one becomes immune to it and understandably learns to build up a protective shield. Otherwise, its 'gaga land' and one does not have a very long career as a caregiver.

His superficial detached expression did not fool me though, and I could tell he was uneasy and sensitive about what he was about to tell me. The bad feeling I had inside me kept growing as he was approaching, and when I shook the sympathetic hand he was extending to me, I felt a painful pinch in the pit of my stomach; every fiber of my being became instantly alert and a definite certitude overcame my whole being. I knew right there and then that we were sealing the final deal.

After the protocolar chitchat was over, he went directly to the point, which I appreciated, for by then I was in no mood for bullshit. "Mr Milot," he said, "I'm sorry to tell you this, but the complete examination and analysis of your wife's lungs shows that, unfortunately, the cancer has spread, which explains the presence of pulmonary liquid. Her condition is so advanced that treatment is not recommended. Further interventions would only add to her pain and discomfort and would lead nowhere. I'm sorry. I recommend that you take her home, and make her comfortable for her remaining days. But the decision is yours since she can't make it herself at this point."

I always believed that no human being should have the power of life and death over another being, human or animal. It is an enormous and overwhelming responsibility and could leave indelible scars on the one making the decision. Yet here I was, burdened with having to decide if Louise should live or die. Even though I knew that it would come to that eventually, I felt extremely inadequate and reluctant to take that step.

After a few light-speed trips around the moon and the worst dizzy spell I ever experienced, I brutally came down to Earth in time to hear myself say: "Yes, doctor. I'll make a few phone calls and arrange to take her back home with me." Then there was silence, deafening silence, and the world around me stood still, frozen in time.

"You don't have to do anything, Mr Milot, I'll make all the arrangements for you. Just go home and take good care of your wife." I heard the distant voice of the doctor bringing me back to reality. "Thank you, doctor," I managed to say with a quivering voice. I then took a couple of deep breaths, turned around to face Alain, Louise's younger brother who had been with me all through that devastating crisis, hugged him tightly, and started to sob.

Who ever said that grown men don't cry? This is BS. I cry and it feels good every time I do. I feel free and liberated as if a weight has been lifted off of my shoulders. That time in the emergency room, although one of the strongest sobbing sessions I ever had, was no different and it helped me unload part of the massive stress afflicting me for the past months. There is something special about sharing pain with another compassionate human being, and hugging my brother-in-law at that crucial moment brought me comfort and strength and made me feel supported. Thanks, Al.

From then on, as promised, I did not have to lift a finger and Louise was taken care of like a princess. Within a few hours, she was resting comfortably at home in a special adapted bed that had been set up for her in our living room.

Our humble *casa* looked more like a deluxe hospital room: leather couch, wet bar (for me), big screen television, and a cute friendly face-licking black cocker spaniel for company. The room was complete with state-of-the-art medical gizmos and of course the inevitable tubes, needles and beeping machines. Nurses and helpers of all kinds were busily hopping around to attend to Louise's every need while a health unit case manager conferred with me to make sure that our patient had everything she needed.

This was all a big surprise to me and I never thought that such an extravaganza could be made available through home care for free. I felt thankful and appreciative. The realization that professionals would now take over Louise's care at home brought about a big sigh of relief on my part, but on the other hand, losing my position as her sole caretaker made me feel off and awkward. Even though I understood that her needs now exceeded my capabilities as a caregiver, I felt that what kept me in close contact with my wife all through these years had been taken away from me. My sense of purpose was gone, and, as I dug deeper into insolation, a profound feeling of loss overcame me; I was not important or needed anymore.

During Louise's increasing dark episodes of mental cloudiness when I could barely communicate with her, I at least had the physical connection brought upon by caring for her. Although my back was not complaining at all and I could start to relax more and sleep a little bit better, this sudden influx of helpers represented one more step ahead in my struggle to learn to let go. Change is hard, especially when it is forced upon you, and this one was a biggy.

Churning and yearning feelings of loss and freedom were thundering guiltily in my chest as, with great reluctance and sorrow, I finally let the truth in; it was over, she was dying and it was only a matter of time before she left me and faded away into a memory. I did not sulk in sadness and self-pity for long though, as I knew darn well that there was still a lot to do. No time for tears now; that would come later, much later I hoped.

From then on my life changed significantly. To say for the better would be a gross exaggeration, but I could at least count on a few well-deserved breaks on a regular basis. A 'sitter' could now come home and stay with Louise while I went out shopping, took a long relaxing car ride, visited the very few friends I had left, or relaxed in the park by the river.

There are always two sides to a medal though and this time was no different. In a way, I should have been happy and appreciative of my newfound freedom, but I felt that this was just another exercise in learning how to live alone as a widower. The good part about anticipatory grief, and its roller-coaster ride of hope and dread, is that one learns to desensitize. One learns to manage emotional pain in small doses, and acceptance of the inevitable becomes a little easier. If the feelings of failure accompanying the downslides have been dealt with successfully throughout, then the rise back from the devastation that loss brings can be shorter and more manageable.

I was far from out of the woods though and I knew it. Well, sort of. I could not fathom at that moment how gruesome and emotionally and physically demanding attending to the needs of a dying loved one may be, but I was about to find out the hard way soon. Granted I did not have to attend to her personal hygiene, toiletries, break my back dragging her around from the couch to the commode as she was now lying in bed permanently, or run up and down the stairs to empty and clean the commode's waste container, for now that she was not on solid food anymore there was nothing to evacuate from her intestine, and her liquid waste was eliminated through a catheter into a plastic bag. I just had to change the bag regularly.

But in spite of the support, there was still a lot to do: helping her change position in bed when it got too uncomfortable, bringing her this and that as needed, massaging her aching back, massaging her hands and feet as they were always cold, sponging her face with a wet towel, and on and on. Well, you know what I mean: all the TLC a husband would do over and above the duties of a regular caregiver.

The medication schedule was simple now: morphine. No more breaking my head administering or struggling to adjust the dosage of the many drugs she was taking which was driving me absolutely nuts. There was a little reprieve there, although the morphine stage represented another fork in the road for me. Three years ago at the beginning of the battle, the drugs were meant to heal her, then to stabilize her and manage her pain, and now they had become an elixir of death. Who has not heard of a terminally ill old uncle, aunt or parent being put on the infamous morphine cocktail, announcing that the end was imminent? Every time I handed Louise the sweet liquid, it ripped my insides and created a rupture in my already screwed-up mind. On the one hand, I felt like the man with the scythe, a traitor presenting a deadly poison, and on the other, a loving being performing a compassionate and mandatory gesture. Morphine, the sweet silent killer they call it. Anybody the least bit familiar with the drug knows that the regular intake of large amounts of it leads to the shutting down of a person's whole metabolism, making the approaching end a not-so-fearful event. I hope there'll be plenty of it around when my time comes.

Cooking and serving her food was also not an issue anymore. In effect, her appetite had declined substantially in the last few months, but now with the morphine, it had disappeared completely; intravenous serum and water were her staple food now.

If noticing the passage of time was not a consideration before, since I was so busy doing a zillion things, now it was a different story. All my newly acquired free time had become my enemy. Staring into space and cogitating on my situation was not helping my growing sense of panic at the thought of being left alone and by myself. What will happen to me? What will happen to her out there, wherever that is? Someone should have been able to tell me to enjoy these few moments of liberty, as my life was about to turn to chaos sooner than expected.

"She has about one week," said the visiting head nurse after examining Louise's deteriorating body. There are signs that a trained health professional can read on a sick person's body which indicate that the system is starting to shut off. From the sequence, the rate of change and the intensity of those indicators, a timeline for the end can be approximatively estimated. Believe it or not, Tibetan monks can read signs of death many months before the end actually arrives. But that's another story; I just felt it appropriate to mention this here.

At this stage, I had donned my emotional armor once more and resumed my automaton attitude. It was the only way I could function properly and not fall to pieces through the intense emotional turmoil I was in. I had to stay sharp, focused and available for Louise's brief occasional moments of clarity. In those instances and like we had done so many times before, we talked about life and the afterlife, her afterlife and my afterlife, what it would be after she was gone. That was her main concern: my safety, my happiness, not hers. What a woman!

Unfortunately, those few instances when she was 'my' Louise had become very scarce and they were reserved just for me. She never wanted to see any of her friends or family who were requesting a visit. "I'm too tired, tell them not to come," she would say. If they did come in spite of that, she could not remain awake for more than a few minutes before returning to her world again. It seemed that she preferred to be there more than here now, like she had already started to make the transition. Some say that before we die, loved ones who have already passed on come to visit and help us prepare for the grand passage. I believe that in Louise's case this was true.

November 2010
Louise's last moment of clarity; a mystical private moment

Acceptance

Her last moment of clarity was a defining moment for me and it will forever be imprinted in my memory.

It was late afternoon and Louise was particularly agitated because of the pain. The morphine doses had been increased to no avail. The administration of the drug went from every four hours to two hours and finally to a one-hour interval and still was not enough. She was moaning and constantly shifting position in her bed. I called the nurse at some point, and she came immediately to assess the situation. Not long after arriving, she decided to call Louise's attending physician to consult on the situation. "Put her on the morphine pump," she instructed the nurse, "and give her a sedative." I could not agree more as, in spite of my phony countenance, I was an emotional wreck and wanted nothing more than to ease Louise's pain.

Preparations were rapidly made and I appreciated how much of an expert the nurse was at this kind of stuff. In a short while, Louise was finally set up with the doomsday machine which started delivering its liquid death immediately. "It will take a little while before she feels the complete effects of the drug and be pain-free though, therefore I will inject her with a powerful sedative so she can calm down in the meantime." The nurse then looked at me with compassionate eyes and said in a soft voice, "When she closes her eyes after this, she may never open them again, so you may want to say your last goodbye." "It's already done," I said, "thank you for caring," and I retreated to the kitchen out of sight to shed a few tears while she was preparing the injection.

After a couple of minutes, as I was returning and passing in front of the living room in order to climb the stairs to the second-floor bathroom, I felt a bizarre sensation, something strange, irresistible and almost supernatural. A little like when you sense somebody poking you on the shoulder in an attempt to get your attention. I could not for the life of me resist the powerful, almost magnetic, attraction to turn my head to the left. The scene offered to my inquisitive eyes can only be described as mystical.

As time seemed to slow down, in a sort of cameo image with its outline all fuzzed up, I saw the bed with its disheveled white sheets, the nurse bending over, busily injecting the sedative in Louise's left leg, and as the scene was becoming more and more defined, I ended up staring straight into Louise's bright intelligent eyes. She had the birth of a smile and seemed slightly amused. I was shocked and could not believe how awakened she seemed. I had goosebumps all over; it was like witnessing a resurrection. As far away and distant as her looks may have been in the last months, I could now see, touch and feel the real Louise through those eyes, my Louise, the way I've always known her, vibrant, loving and caring. It was like coming back home. As our eyes locked in for a brief instant (which actually seemed more like an eternity), I became transfixed and mesmerized and I saw, as in a mental movie screen, our life together unfolding at lightning speed, a sort of request from her to remember, never to forget who we were, our love, our pains, our hopes. I was elated, flabbergasted and sad all at the same time and, with the deadliest of certainty, I knew she was saying her last goodbye. Then, coming out of my trance, the world around me came alive again, clocks started ticking once more and this extraordinary blissful moment disappeared as fast as it had appeared. With great sadness, I watched her slowly close her beautiful eyes, reluctantly accepting that she would never open them again.

Louise's last hours

My special moment occurred around three o'clock in the afternoon, and after the nurse left when the drug had finally taken effect, everything went dead silent in the house. I was alone with Louise, who was sleeping comfortably and pain-free, a fact I appreciated a lot, a whole lot. I could now let my guard down and relax a bit, well, relax as much as it is possible to relax when you're lying on a couch watching your wife die. I had gone through a roller-coaster ride of emotions previously and I was ready for a break; boy, was I ever. I was exhausted; every muscle in my body ached as if I had lost a fight against a grizzly bear. All kinds of feelings and weird emotions were pouring out of my being like hot lava rushing down the side of a volcano, my heart pounding. I could not sleep or eat, and the only liquid permitted to slide down my dry throat was my buddy Mr Scotch. Bring it on, keep it coming.

I don't really know how long I stayed there vegging out and drinking, but I felt better, a lot better. I took a look at Louise, who had not moved an inch since she had closed her eyes and although this 'doing nothing' thing felt good, I knew something was meant to happen eventually. Will she move again, will she moan in pain? How many days will this last? I wonder when she dies if her eyes will remain closed or open in a blank stare. Will I be able to close them like they do in movies? What's gonna happen next, when will the nurse be back…? A zillion questions were popping up in my troubled mind. I felt alone and neglected. Louise's body was there, but for some reason, I knew that her spirit had gone. There was an emptiness in the room that was not there before. I really did not know what to do. Wait? Wait for what? The nurse said there would be signs, but what signs? Hell, this was all new to me. Who the heck knows what to do with a dying person. I'd never done this before. This nonsense must have been going on for an hour when all of a sudden I heard a gurgling sound coming from Louise. Curious, I looked at her; nothing, nothing noticeable at least. Then I heard it again. It sounded like someone trying to breathe through a congested nose full of mucus. I stood up and went to investigate closer. I could not see anything, but I could hear the disturbing sound on and off when she exhaled. All was normal, at least in the conventional sense, but maybe not so normal since she was a dying person, but then again, maybe it's normal for a dying person to emit bizarre noises. "What the hell, will you let it go and relax, Pierre?" I thought, sat back down and resumed ruminating while keeping a curious eye on Louise.

Thirty minutes had passed and just when I thought I was off the hook, there it went again: that awful noise was back with a vengeance, and this time when I looked, there was a horrible thick greyish substance coming out of her nose. I immediately went to the rescue and wiped it clean. Then everything went quiet again and, thinking that it was just a freak incident, feeling a little disgusted I sat back down on the leather couch and cleaned my hands. Little did I know then that this was just the tip of the iceberg.

Another 30 minutes or so had passed and there it went again:

the gurgling sound; I stood up, grabbed a kleenex, squeezed Louise's nose between my index and my thumb, pulled down gently to excrete the mucus into the kleenex, dropped the soiled tissue in the garbage can beside her bed, made sure she was breathing properly, washed my hands and walked back to crash on the couch.

I looked at the clock wondering if and when it would happen again. It had been almost 25 minutes since the last episode and just as soon as I thought about it, there it goes, that ghastly sound again. I stood up one more time, grabbed another kleenex and (well, you know the rest...).

When this horrific little scenario had occurred steadily for the last couple of hours, in some sort of, well, I couldn't call it panic, but it was close, I decided to contact the nurse to come to my rescue. It was around 6 p.m. when she arrived, 30 minutes after I had called her, and I was damn glad to see her. She was the same one that gave Louise the injection that put her out; a young slim good-looking woman who played her part to perfection and, from my past experience with her, she was as professional as she looked. I started to breathe more easily the minute she walked through the door. *Finally, somebody to tell me what to do*, I thought, and cutting short on the politeness I informed her of the situation.

Obviously, she had seen this before as she didn't even bat an eye at my predicament. After an all-around check-up of the many tubes and wires connected to Louise showed no faults, she proceeded to examine her hands and feet and listened for a while to Louise's breathing. After writing a bunch of notes in a thick white binder, she looked at me straight in the eyes and with a detached voice said, "If you have to call someone, I would do it now if I were you because it will be over sooner than expected." A week had turned to days and days had turned to hours and Louise was fading fast. I think she had been ready to go for a while and that after her parting smile, her soul partly gone, her body had become nothing else but a deteriorating corpse.

"As the final moment approaches," the nurse said, "her toes and fingernails will become blue and her breathing will become labored and irregular. Well, you'll know when it happens. Please call me when it's over," she said and without preamble she left. It must be hard to keep at arm's distance from your patients when you are a caring caregiver, and I closed the door to a silent house. It was Louise and I alone again (or the part of her that was left anyway). I could not believe that after 38 years of togetherness, it had come to this already, and deeply distressed, I sat back down on the couch and cried a river.

I called everyone I had to, and they were few and far apart. Sadly, my family hadn't shown much interest in Louise and me, in the three years that she was sick, so I didn't call them, and the few friends that Louise allowed to come had visited already. There were only her three brothers left, and when I reached them, they promised to come.

As I stood a faithful vigil, determined to see this to the end, I witnessed the episodes of the chilling 'death rattle' (terminal respiratory secretions) become more and more frequent. I knew about this now as I had researched the phenomenon in quiet times between incidents. Apparently 'terminal secretion' is normal and occurs frequently with dying people. I was a bit pissed off at the nursing staff to not have informed me earlier of this. I would not have panicked so much; I would not have spent so much nervous energy worrying about what in blazes was going on with Louise.

Learning about the death rattle also answered some of the questions that were rolling through my overloaded mind: what would have happened to Louise if I would have placed her in a hospital to end her days? How would this 'mucus thing' have been dealt with? Would the busy medical staff have left her alone in a dark room, allowing the thick liquid to drip into a container? Would they have drained the mucus directly from her throat, which I heard could be very uncomfortable for the patient? All these questions may sound weird and ridiculous to a trained professional, but to me, a novice in this sort of thing, they were all legitimate concerns and they should have been addressed at the proper time by the medical staff; I should have known. This was a major mishap.

All this pondering made me realize, though, that I had made the right decision about taking care of Louise at home till the end. No one in a public facility, hospital or hospice would have given her the same level of care as I did. Nobody would have wiped her nose clean during and after each gurgling episode, nobody would have wet her dry lips and sponged her pale greyish forehead with as caring a hand as mine, nobody would have sat by the side of her bed reassuringly holding her cold dying hand while whispering encouragingly in her ear, "You're doing fine, honey, I'm here with you, baby. Follow the light, there'll be people you know waiting for you there. I love you with all my heart. Don't worry about me, sweetie, I'll be fine." No one. Absolutely no one could have been as supportive and comforting, and I felt privileged to be there with and for her in such an important time in her life. All my aches and pains were well worth my efforts and I would have done it all over again if I had to.

It was 10 p.m. and the rattle was almost constant now. I asked Al, Louise's younger brother who had arrived an hour earlier, to replace me for a while so I could take a break. As he took over the daunting task, I stood aside reluctantly and got busy observing Louise's breathing which had become very labored by this time. Her breaths were short and shallow with long pauses between each one. Every time I thought she would not breathe in again, she would surprise me with a sudden and noisy intake of air and the process would start all over again.

While all of this was happening, I was wondering impatiently what Louise's other brothers were doing. I was worried that if they didn't arrive soon, she'd be gone, they'd miss her departure.

Then, 15 minutes into my break, the rattling seemed to have disappeared completely, which was a real blessing for me as my nerves were raw; I was exhausted and had become very irritated by the eerie gurgling sound. I was also maintaining a constant state of slight nausea even though I had not eaten a bite for hours. Nothing to do now than listen patiently to the rhythm of her breath, which had become the only determinant factor left in trying to establish some kind of timeline for her transition. Helplessly watching Louise fading away was crushing and guilt-ridden, as one part of me wanted it to be over while the other was still hanging on, not quite ready to let go of her yet.

Suddenly, after another short while, I heard a soft knock on the door and Andre, Louise's second brother, walked in through the front door, letting at the same time the outside world intrude briefly on our sanctuary. He was apparently stressed out and eager to find out if he had made it in time. "I was detained," he said in a faint voice as if afraid to disturb the intimacy of the scene offered to him. "I reached Claude (the oldest of her brothers), and he can't make it," he whispered. "It's OK," I mouthed and waved him in. Nothing else was said. It wasn't necessary; we all knew what was coming. The atmosphere in the death room was heavy and filled with veiled emotions and remembrances. The deafening silence was perturbed only by Louise's subtle breathing which had become nothing else but a sigh at this point.

All of a sudden, as if by some mysterious intervention, in unison we all became aware that our beloved's departure was imminent. We then reflexively grouped up over Louise's body; Andre lovingly touching his sister's arm, Alain bending his head trying unsuccessfully to hide his pain, and I sitting by her side joining my trembling hand with hers, witnessed Louise passing away peacefully in a long, long soft sigh. It was finally over. She was gone forever.

With tears rolling down my cheeks, I kissed her delicate hair that surprisingly still carried her particular scent I loved so much, closed her eyelids gently with a brush of my hand and, with a broken heart, I said goodbye to my baby for the last time. It was November 28th, midnight, a time to be remembered.

Chapter 12

Post-Loss:
September to December 2011
Creating a new life
Building new relationships, meeting new friends, experiencing separation anxiety

Christine: my life takes a whole new turn

Christine is a very good-looking 63-year-old woman with a cute turned-up nose and a devastating smile. She shows off a slim, healthy silhouette which makes her the envy of other women and has men execute a double-take just to glance at her a second time. She has the 'it factor,' some inexplicable attractive aura and an inborn ability to stand out like a star. She is often compared to Elizabeth Taylor, for instance. One can simply not ignore her charm and the glamorous way she has about her. She is a sharp dresser and I can't count (to my surprise) the times she's been hailed on the street by admirers impressed by her pizzazz. She is a retired school teacher, a business woman and a writer among her many talents. The way she wears her reading glasses low on her nose gives her a lovely scholarly look and she behaves in a reserved and distinguished manner, except for the private times when she brings on her kidding side. She is the perfect host and socialite, a quality I appreciate since I'm the exact opposite, so we balance each other out very well. We have a lot in common which is great, but we also have somewhat different views of what life should be or shouldn't be and we debate our views with gusto at times. Now let me tell you how it all began.

Let's meet for coffee

There are different kinds of grief. Mine is called 'anticipatory' because of the emotional roller-coaster ride I underwent during the many periods of remission and relapses that Louise suffered through her long period of sickness. The ups I experienced when Louise was apparently healing and the downs I sank into when the cancer came back made my 'skin thicker', so to speak, and forced me to adapt more quickly which accelerated my grieving timeline. Also, my many years of practice as a trained stress management therapist enhanced greatly my abilities to dig myself out of the hole.

It's only been seven months since I became a widower; I am in the last grieving stage and it's time for me to meet new people and make new friends. It's a must if I want to restructure my life in this new world without Louise. I'm alone and isolated in my little country home now, and aside from my family and my dog Max, who's not much of a talker, I'm not in contact with many people. It's kind of OK, I guess, for the semi-loner that I always was, but the 'new me' needs more, I decide. Contemplating male bonding through various men's social clubs does not appeal to me; playing cards, bocce, horse shoe or drinking beer in bars while watching sports is not my style. So what's left, I ask myself one day, and the answer is quick to come: female compan-ionship. Whoa, whoa, stop that right now, I know what you're thinking, but my intentions are pure, I assure you. Let's face it, when it comes to spending quality time with a person, I'd rather opt for the female gender with all its soft and gentle attributes than a robust 'beer-bellied-hairy-chested' dude. I much prefer a brainy exchange with a smart (and cute if possible) woman over a pissing contest with a bunch of macho guys to prove my manhood. Don't get me wrong, I know many men with a brain, and exchanging with them would be interesting and challenging, but they only have one problem: they're men.

Meeting interesting people is not as easy as one might think, especially if that person has to respond to certain requirements; must be a woman of course, be of average height, preferably blonde but any hair color will do, have blue or green eyes, be slim, educated, have a marked interest for a healthy lifestyle, a sense of humor, and must absolutely love music and dogs, the works, what! Well, if I have to choose, I may as well be picky, right? And in the off chance that this friend relationship turns more serious, is it not better to cover my tracks and fill my basic needs and desires?

Cruising bars, social dance clubs and gyms offers very limited options and furthermore they cost quite a bit of money. Internet dating sites on the other hand are more practical, cheaper, and provide a lot more advantages. As someone once told me, it's like browsing through a shopping list, easy and fun. Although I never gave them too much credit (my assumption was that they were for losers or out-of-luck ugly ducklings) I, nevertheless, have heard of very happy couples who swear that they are together because of them.

I decide to give it a shot. After a quick research of the many sites available, I rest my choice on 'Plenty of Fish' (POF), one of the easiest and most popular on the market. Registration is a bit cumbersome but I get over it eventually (photo, personality profile and all that jazz), pay my fees, press the submit button and I'm on the market, one more fish in the sea of love. I feel a bit foolish to do this though, but hey, what do I have to lose? One who risks nothing gains nothing, right? Little did I know then that *moi* and my 'apparent irresistible charm' (I'm only relaying here what a few girls once told me) would attract more than a few bites.

I'm not a bad-looking chap and I demonstrate quite a few interesting attributes for a *belle* looking for a *beau*, and it isn't long before destiny rings my bell. I am not necessarily looking for a long-term relationship and I made that clear when I filled out my profile. But I am also not closing the door for something more serious should the situation arise. My goal is mainly to meet female friends with whom I have an affinity, someone I can share intelligent and challenging conversations with, spend some quality time with; a little dining and dancing, movies, concerts, etc., take it from there and let the relationship evolve naturally. In the end all I want is to alleviate my loneliness and realign my life in a new direction.

Deep inside though, I'm concerned that I could subconsciously be looking for a replacement for Louise, a compensation for the immense emptiness she left me in. In that sense, my search could be more for a life partner than a friend, which is OK I guess as long as it doesn't become 'love on the rebound.' I admit that there is danger there and I must not fall into that trap; it wouldn't be fair for her and for me.

'Meet them over coffee' is the dating expert's recommendation. This way, if it doesn't work out, you're only looking at 30 minutes of suffering and the price of an espresso (the guys always pay of course) instead of busting your monthly 'Casanova' budget on a possible boring, long two-hour dinner on someone you barely know or want to know. That's assuming you followed the protocol of first contacts by e-mail and phone to size out if you're in sync and speak the same language, at least.

First meet: hypothetical situation

Then the day of the meet finally arrives. As you stand in anticipation in front of the java shop, you suddenly see a car pull up in the parking lot and, trying to look cool, you immediately shift your eyes (not your head, as it has to remain steady and show a face exhibiting an air of indifference) to take a curious peek at the driver to see if it's your date. No chance, the tinted windows won't let you, but your curiosity is satisfied as soon as you see the shape of a female body slowly move out of the vehicle, stand up, peruse the area to locate a handsome-looking guy, and once her radar shifts towards you, she starts walking in your direction, praying hard that her date is not in fact the bald fat dude wearing blue shorts, a yellow t-shirt and multi-colored running shoes standing on the other side of the door, also waiting for his *belle*. What can I say, coffee shops on Sunday mornings are a well-known meet place for expectant first daters.

Your heart skips a beat, at first in excitement in the face of the unknown, but too often in disillusionment, for as she approaches, you realize disappointingly that the photo of the person you saw displayed on the site does not match the actual individual in front of you. Some have become 'blimps' since their photo was taken (how can they hope to get away with such a scam, do they think we're blind, or worse, idiots?), or they have added a thousand wrinkles on their tired face and look like your grand-mother. *Oh God*, you think, *please help me find a way out of this one, please, pretty please.* Then, prayer turns rapidly into anger at the same God for playing this nasty stunt on you to start with. *We'll have to talk later, God!* you think, as panic starts to set in.

Stuck in that moment in time, your problem-solving mind sparks out of control, trying desperately to find a way out. The minutes fly by at an indescribable speed and, frozen on the spot, you question your sanity for being there. You wonder if running, even at the cost of looking like a coward, wouldn't be better than sitting and chatting for an 'eternity' (or so it seems) with Mother Earth. Time elapses rapidly, and soon, backed up against the wall, the only thing left for you to do is to paint a superficial smile on your sorry face, tend a reluctant hand and say with faked enthusiasm: "How are you...? Hi, my name is Pierre... etc." *It's gonna be a long hour*, you think as you watch your timepiece crawling at turtle pace already. "Dammit, I've been had...again," you mumble to yourself as you enter the crowded bistro.

Why do I know all this stuff, you will ask? Because I've been there too many times. Why is it so? Are people so desperate to meet someone that they have to bend the truth, or even outright lie? I mean, not all the ladies I've met are like that, of course, and I spend some quality time with many of them. It just does not work out, that's all; no synergy, no attraction, not on the same page, etc.

And then you have the other kind of women, and my quest to find a healthy lifestyle enthusiast got me into trouble more than once with those, the extreme sport aficionados. For them (they look pretty normal, you know; how am I to know, although their sinewy musculature should give me an indication?), the term 'taking a walk' holds a very different meaning for them than for me. Going out on a date with these girls equals risking my life, as I often find myself in crazy off-the-charts situations: cross-country walking (almost jogging would be a more adequate term) for miles in rugged scruffy terrain or recklessly climbing steep scary mountains, almost herniating my over-stressed groin muscles in the process, all the while doing my best to exhibit a cool composure in an effort to hide my fear of heights. Maybe they're just trying me out to gauge what kind of material I'm made of. Boy, what would a man not do to impress a girl? At times my heart beats so fast, I'm afraid of croaking from a heart attack, which would make me lose face and be embarrassing, well, hum…not really since I'd be dead and therefore would not care. My heirs on the other hand might, and I hope they would not seek revenge on me for the embarrassment I've caused them by engraving my mortuary monument with the nasty epitaph: 'Our dad, died of cardiac arrest trying to impress a girl.' This is not exactly the way I want to be remembered.

"Sorry that I can't stay too long. My old dog is very sick and I need to go tend to him, poor Max," I often say in a desperate effort to whizz out of my sorry predicaments. It's my favorite line and it works. Each time it gets me the exit I need and I run out of there like a bat out of hell. I'm sure though that some of them don't really believe my fabrications and scratch me off their list of available tough dudes. Ten gone, none to go. "Where have all the real men gone?" they scream. "Gone to have a quiet coffee with a normal woman," I answer.

Attraction on the rebound

So it goes for many months, and I must admit my involvement in an on-and-off convoluted summer romance with 'K', a 50-year-old blue-eyed girl with frizzy blonde hair and an emotional disposition as sinuous as her shapely athlete's body. The course is rocky and full of obstacles; irreconcilable differences, as they say in divorce courts. The doomed-from-the-start relationship is not working well and I think I may be on the rebound, a dangerous ground to tread on and an unfair situation for both of us. But the relationship is not all that bad, and I must admit that it has its good moments at times, even if 'K' drags me mountain climbing a little too often for my taste. On the positive side though, the roller-coaster struggle I go through while dating her helps me mature in my grief, grow stronger emotionally and understand myself a little better, something I'm grateful for as it represents the first real steps I'm forced to take to redefine my life. But nevertheless, this unhealthy relationship has to end; I just don't know how or when. For now, I will carry it on and off as usual until the opportunity to break it off definitively arises. I will need a strong incentive though, and little do I know at this stage that the opportunity will present itself later on in the summer when 'C's profile will appear on the dating website.

All through the summer in the off periods from 'K', I date like there's no tomorrow. It's one phone call after the other; e-mails and text messages with prospective dates come and go like in a telemarketing call center. I'm having the time of my life and this routine helps me to ignore my pain. It would already be awesome should it only help me alleviate my loneliness, but I'm also hoping that it could be instrumental in building up the network of acquaintances and friends I desperately need to restart my new life.

Unfortunately though, as I find out as the months pass, rejected ex-dates don't appreciate being ignored or discarded. Most become put off, unfriendly and stop answering my phone calls and e-mails, so in the end, I find myself alone again. *Is all this really worth it?* I wonder. *Maybe I should trust faith and hang loose for a while, maybe I'll bump into someone and it'll be it. Maybe I'm not meant to meet anybody and doomed to spend the rest of my days as a single, which wouldn't be that bad after all, I could adapt,* I cogitate as I peruse another page from the website with less and less interest.

Over the months, I find it's not so much fun anymore; I'm discontented and irritated with my weird relationship with 'K' and I'm tired of the tedious and shallow encounters that the dating site provides me. I'm seriously thinking of dropping the whole thing and shutting down the site for good, when all of a sudden, a notification appears on my computer screen: 'a new profile has just been added to your favorites list, click here to go to her page.' Curious, but not all that enthusiastic as I've been through this so many times before, I click the link and her profile shows up. The very little that her picture reveals looks good, her psychological profile is interesting and in line with my search, and as a 'cherry on the sundae,' as they say, she lives in the neighboring town 20 minutes away from me. Great. Let's give it a shot, but it's the last time I'm doing this. If that doesn't work out, I'm done. *Que sera sera.*

So here we go one last time with the e-mail routine; no phone calls this time as I lack motivation now. It went wrong so many times before, this one is just a last ditch effort. From the start it looks like it's gonna crash; every time I come up with a time and date for a meet, she e-mails back with a negative, she proposes another option, and it's not convenient for me, and so on and so forth, until finally after a lengthy exchange over the net, we agree to meet for coffee at the Alexandria Restaurant at ten o'clock Sunday morning.

Immediately after finalizing the meet, I sense that my life has just taken a new turn. I can feel it in my guts. She's different from all the other ones before; there's a familiarity about her. It excites me but I can't put my finger on it.

Now tomorrow is not just another day. Where will all this lead me? I can't wait to see.

Sunday, September 18, 2011
The beginning of my new life

It's 10 a.m. and I have been at the *rendezvous* point earlier as usual, and I'm pacing discreetly, close to the entrance of the Alexandria Restaurant, waiting for my date. Right on time, I see a brown-reddish two-door Jeep Wrangler pull into the parking lot and as I watch the vehicle stop and park, I'm not entirely sure if I want it to be her. A Jeep? Is she one of those adventurous ones again? Please no, I've had enough. No more nerve-wrecking, back-breaking outings with muscular girls; been there, done that. If she's like that, I may as well pack it in and run back home right now, I conclude as I observe her disembarking her slim body out of the car. She turns around and walks towards me as she adjusts the pale brown short leather jacket she's wearing over a pair of molding dark brown leather pants that reveal a set of tight hips, a cute *derrière* as they say in French, and a cowboy hat and boots to match. Mmm, lovely, I purr with satisfaction. But my wits are not to be deterred that easily by this delightful temptress and I remain on my guard. What if she's into this horseback-riding stuff? Whoa. Hold your skittles, buddy, better be careful and don't jump to conclusions. I try desperately to peek through her dark sunglasses to get a glimpse of her eyes.

She walks with a confidence that only winners possess, and in an instant 'C' stands in front of me, gives me a Colgate smile and says: "Pierre? Are you looking for someone?" A bit stunned I say, "Ahhh…Yes. Are you Christine?" I answer back feeling a bit soft in the coconut. Who else but her would be here to meet you, you nutcase? Nevertheless, she gratifies me with the obvious positive answer and, at that moment, I seriously start to worry. Is being weak in the knees a sign of something?

If she's sizing me up, she's good at it, for she remains stone-faced, dignified and cool, and doesn't let out the tiniest little sign of an insecurity she surely also feels. Spontaneously, we shake hands, I extend a polite and inviting arm towards the door, and I follow her inside as I enjoy the view; it doesn't hurt to look, right? Once inside, we choose a table way back in a discreet corner and away from the crowd so we can have an intimate conversation.

We've been sitting and getting acquainted for close to five minutes when she finally decides to take off her darn sunglasses, and wham, I'm bedazzled and frozen on the spot, as a set of mesmerizing blue eyes stares right at me and deep within my soul. I'm instantly seduced, cooked, fried and I feel myself melting by the minute. Any attempt to escape (why should I for heaven's sake, but then again, panic will make you behave in strange ways) would be futile at this point as my butt is glued to the chair and my legs are paralyzed in bewilderment. Control yourself, you fool. She mustn't have even the slightest hint of your discombobulation. I keep repeating to myself, breathe in, breathe out. Relax. Ask her questions; make her talk about herself while you recuperate.

But what I didn't know then (she will confess to this later) is that my 'green Zen monk-like' eyes (as she calls them) were having a similar effect on her. God forbid she would have let out a single clue of her disturbances. No way; Ms 'Cool' was imperturbable and continued to rattle my cage mercilessly. Two players in the mating game.

The attraction I feel for Christine is multi-dimensional though, and not just physical. Being close to her instills in me a sense of *déjà vu*, a delightful familiarity as if I'd be recognizing a loved one lost in a time passed. Karma? Reincarnation? When her blue penetrating eyes stare into mine, it's as if she reaches into the confines of my being and reawakens old sentiments buried deep in the past. There has to be a karmic link between the two of us, and I'll be more convinced of that as I will learn from her later on, that after a prolonged absence from the dating site, she had decided for no particular reason to momentarily allow her profile to be viewed at the precise moment I perused the site one last time and stumbled on her. Coincidence? I think not. The whole situation throws me off considerably, a condition I'm not accustomed to.

Eventually, I get a hold of myself and the conversation starts to flow. We talk of this and that, our likes and dislikes, our goals, our professional life experiences, etc. We even find out that we're both medicinal clay eaters (taking a spoonful of clay each morning is an efficient liver-cleansing method, and even if you think it's weird, it does work marvelously), a rarity these days, which gives us an important edge in the compatibility area. We also brush quickly on the subject of our spouses (ex-husband in her case and late wife in mine), but when it comes to our children, things get a bit touchy as I have lost a son 28 years ago and Christine has lost two sons, one of whom just passed away three months ago, so we don't expand on that too much for now, maybe later. But nevertheless, it puts us on familiar ground and helps us understand each other a little bit better, a huge plus in our favor.

Contrary to my other coffee dates, where I kept looking at my watch to gauge how many minutes my torture would last, time passes quickly and too soon I hear Christine say: "I'm so sorry, I've got to run, I'm late already for my volunteer work at the Dunvegan Museum." We then stand up to leave, but even in her haste I feel she is hesitant to depart, while as for me, I could easily hang out with her endlessly and I'm sorry to see her go, a very good sign.

We agree to see each other soon, but make no definite plans about it. The day passes smoothly and I'm walking on a cloud, happy but perplexed nevertheless. This morning's experience was quite unusual and leaves me wondering what the heck is going on. I want to know more about this woman. So after dinner

I call her to suggest we take a leisurely stroll in old Montreal the next day, maybe a little dinner and definitely a lot of chatting.

"Yes, I'd be delighted to go with you," she answers immediately (no hesitation, wow, cool). We talk on the phone for quite a while, and to close our conversation, we agree on a time and a place where I'm to pick her up. I can't wait.

It's Monday 10 a.m. and I'm pulling into the parking lot of the condo complex to wait for Christine. On time, I see her coming out of the side door wearing a neat pair of sunglasses (her signature look, I'll come to realize later) and holding a bunch of unidentified objects in her hands and looking like a Hollywood movie star. I think I like this. I come out of the car, open the door for her and, as I help her in, I realize that among other gizmos, she's holding a cordless home telephone. "What's this?" I ask half-puzzled and half-jokingly. "Oops," she says, "I do that sometimes," as she puts the handset on the back seat. Ms Cool, not flinching an inch on the embarrassment scale, says with all the ease in the world, "I need a sweeper, you know, someone to pick up stuff after me. I tend to lose things. Do you want the job?" she asks with a teasing smile. "Ahh...yes, sure," I answer back, and at that crucial moment I had absolutely no clue of what the heck I was getting into.

We've been driving for a short while when Christine starts to experience a hot flash, or power surge as she calls it, and takes off her leather jacket. I'd like to think that her reaction has to do with my hot sensual body, but as I will learn later she tends to be like that, darn it. Underneath, she's wearing a sleeveless blouse that reveals a good part of her arms and neck, nothing very special in the garment department, quite reserved actually, but to me it has an incredible effect.

I mean, am I weird or what? We've all heard talks about sexy body parts: thighs, waist, navel, belly, hips, back, etc. But arms? Who the hell considers arms to be sexy? I do evidently, and I'm thrown off at the sight of Christine's. She has the most gorgeous upper arms I've ever seen; her skin looks soft and is slightly tanned with a few freckles here and there. I swear to you, if it would not be for the fear of making a fool of myself, grrr, I could just grab her left one and have a go at it with kisses and love bites.

One can only picture the ridiculous sight: me, steering the car recklessly while chewing on my unfortunate passenger's arm pulled out in front of my mouth, and Christine screaming in panic and beating on my head with her purse. Man, that would surely jeopardize my chances of another date, wouldn't it?

I can treat myself to some imaginings, can't I? As we go along on our ride I have to make constant efforts to keep my eyes on the road and not on Christine's yummy arms. The day goes swimmingly. The weather cooperates with glorious sunshine and a gentle breeze and Christine's arms look more delicious than ever. We walk lazily through the narrow streets and alleyways of Old Montreal, appreciating the beauty of the antique buildings and port area as we get further acquainted. We have a succulent dinner together in a French restaurant (she loves the French culture and food; one strike for me as I'm French) and we drive back home, both reluctant to see the day end.

Back at my house, after this wonderful day, I cannot help but reflect on how my life has changed since Louise has gone, how I went from hell to heaven, depression to motivation, from wishing to die to wanting to live in such a short amount of time. As I relax, sitting on my veranda sipping a glass of wine, even though I am content, I feel a mounting sadness overwhelming me, and a tear rolls down my cheek. Will I ever be free of the underlying sting of my losses? Can I put all the pain behind me? Will I ever be able to live, appreciate beauty and fall in love again in spite of my sufferings? I wonder. But thankfully, the blissful moments I had today with Christine reinstate my faith in the idea that a better and happier future is possible for me. Hope I'm right.

During the following days I don't feel or have the inclination to see or talk to other women and I decide to hold back my communications with all of my prospective dates. Christine left a huge impression on me and I can't get her out of my head. Actually, I don't want to as the thought of her keeps me walking on a cloud, a wonderful sensation I savor preciously, until...

It's 11 a.m. and a phone ring brings me out of my reveries. Not wanting to chat with anyone in fear that my elation will disappear, I nevertheless take a peek at the caller ID just in case it would be *ma belle* calling to reveal her mad and eternal love for me, but my joy rapidly turns into disillusion as I realize that it is K's voice instead. "I miss you and I want to make up," she cries. "I've been thinking about us and I think we can make it work," she insists. "Why don't you come over for the weekend and we'll talk about it?" In an effort to be respectful, I try to break it up gently to her by describing my new relationship with Christine.

Not easy to deter, K fires back in anguish, "Why don't you try her out for a couple of days and then come spend the weekend with me and compare?" Suddenly, my plate is full and I decide that that's it for me. I explained that I wouldn't be comfortable doing that. "We're over. Please don't call me back." And with that, I hung up.

After the fumes coming out of my ears have evaporated a bit, I ring Christine up and invite her to dinner at my place: "How would you like to have sushi and sake for dinner at my humble abode *ce soir*?" I ask my lady. "Wonderful!" she enthuses without hesitation. "What can I bring?" she asks. "Just you and your delightful personality," I answer. *I'd luuuv to have you for dessert though*, I think, but I prefer to keep that thought to myself.

As I had hoped, the night goes smoothly, the cool jazz music mix I have chosen sets the perfect romantic mood, the food is superb, and in a mock play, we compliment the chef, *moi*, and Christine even gratifies me with a sweet kiss on the cheek in appreciation for the lovely dinner. All in all, it's a winner and I score high on the 'possible next date' scale.

As she prepares to drive back to her place, we promise to

keep in touch as often as possible. But as I watch her leaving, turning around and blowing me a kiss from the open window of her car as a departing gesture, I experience an odd sensation in the pit of my stomach: I miss her already. The space she leaves behind is reminiscent of a familiar feeling that almost killed me not long ago. I get this nondescript fear rapidly creeping in on me; like Louise did, Christine could leave me too. I feel the panic rising. Relax, bud, I tell myself, trying to make light of the situation. You don't even know if she really wants to see you again, you twit. Take it one day at a time, I remind myself and reaffirm the old Zen saying, 'Tomorrow will take care of tomorrow.' For now enjoy your day and please don't think about it anymore; actually, get out of your head and don't 'think' at all.

Is the same night soon enough to reach out to my possibly-soon-to-be new girlfriend? No, but let me explain. You see, I always suffered from insomnia, and my ability to hit the pillow soundly has diminished considerably through the three years I took care of Louise. The continuous vigil by her side in order to attend to her many needs made a chronic insomniac out of me. I'm lucky if I sleep two to three hours in one night.

Anyway, to make a long story short, tonight is no different from any other night and at four o'clock in the morning, after roaming aimlessly around the house, I decide to send an e-mail to Christine. Just a word to say hello. What's the harm in it? After all, she'll read it only when she gets up in the morning. It's not more than five minutes since I sent my e-mail when I hear a 'ding' on my computer announcing the arrival of a new message, and guess what? It's Christine answering me back. Wide awake also, she had been pacing the rug of her apartment, a habit of hers as she also suffers from insomnia. Here's something special to discover about each other, one more thing in common that we have, I gladly observe. If we make it to old age together, maybe we'll trade sleeping pills and painkillers, or maybe we'll gulp a little shot of brandy to help knock us out faster. But I'm getting ahead of myself here, let's take care of today first, well...hum...tonight, that is, and *ma belle* and *moi* went on chatting on the internet for a while. We finally ended our nocturnal interlude by agreeing to meet a couple of days later at the Dunvegan Museum to watch the 1812 War re-enactment.

An awkward moment

The museum is charming with all its old buildings, carefully reproduced in the style of the era. Worn-out log cedar fences, mock army encampment filled with soldiers neatly dressed up in their 1812 epoch garments and carrying carbines bearing long bayonets. Nothing I haven't seen before, but what makes this place so special is that she's here, somewhere, to meet me. Eventually, my visual search bears fruits and I see her coming out of a cozy little square log cabin that serves as an administrative office.

I don't know why, but sometimes there are images that stick into your head; more often than not, they have no significance at all, but still your mind fixates on them. For me it's the striking image of Christine walking out of that building, and I strongly feel that this moment will be one of those memorable ones.

As I observe her coming down the stairs I feel a thump in my chest and I'm so glad to see her. She's wearing a short grey-greenish skirt over a pair of black stretch pants, a white blouse covered by a sleeveless linen vest, and a gentle breeze tousles her dark brown curly hair. Her head is bent and she seems very absorbed in reading a white piece of paper she's holding in her hands, and I think: *Look ahead, baby, look where you're going, you might trip, fall and hurt yourself.* No sooner has that thought come to me, than she looks up straight at me, waves and starts walking in my direction, giving me a big beautiful smile.

We spend the day enjoying the numerous exhibits, the old log buildings, and Christine takes great pleasure in describing to me the place and its history. While we wait for the show to begin, we decide to go take a walk in the nearby cemetery, as we both think it is a peaceful place and not as creepy as commonly believed. We sit on a bench sheltered by a big maple tree and chat for a while, unknowingly dirtying our clothes with bird poo and tree sap, one for posterity. But the day isn't over yet and another awkward situation lies ahead of me.

When the time comes to watch the war re-enactment, we line up at the gate waiting for the show to begin. As I discreetly try to erase the bird crap artwork decorating my butt, I am discombobulated by an impromptu, hum…how shall I say, ah…family/ex-family reunion? "Pierre," Christine says casually, "please meet my son 'B' and 'M' his girlfriend and 'D and D', my ex-husband and his wife." *Gulp and double gulp,* I react silently. *What the heck?* I shake everybody's hand (paying special attention to the 'ex' while I assess him quickly), feeling a little weird and out of place. The fact that no one engages me in conversation adds to my discomfort. *Hum…* I think and I leave it at that. Little did I know then that feeling a bit off and out of place at times is a sensation that will nibble at me sporadically all through my voyage into my new life.

Another day passes and I'm more and more into Christine. My feelings of vulnerability increase as I progressively let down my guard in order to fit into her world. *I sure hope she feels the same way about me,* I reflect. I'm reluctant to give in, more out of fear of being hurt and abandoned should the relationship not be successful.

That I'm afraid of being left alone again is understandable, as the loss of Louise left a deep scar, but the abandonment part is new to me. Where does that come from? I should meditate on that. Man, discovering the new me sure has its fun side, but I'm more and more concerned that the can of worms it opens up at the same time may bring me back down into the manure hole again. Nevertheless, I must not let fear deter me from my goal. I must not dwell on how things could be or couldn't be. Still your mind and enjoy the ride, I prime myself. My tomorrows are made of my todays. If my todays are filled with worries, my tomorrows will reflect that and I'll only add to my misery, a real Catch 22. Don't think, just be.

Before parting for the day, Christine invites me to the interment of her son Damon, which is to take place the next day in the Maxville cemetery. "But of course I'll be there," I answer quickly, more than happy to be with her one more time. I'm a little surprised to be invited for such a private moment so early in our relationship though.

Burial day; a disheartening moment

The day is hot, I mean stinking hot, the kind of day that solar panel owners wish for: a deep blue sky from which emanates burning sun rays transforming the air into a scorching inferno. The numbers on the thermometer must be climbing over 35 degrees Celsius, or so it feels to me, as I'm wearing my Hugo Boss black summer wool suit, a crisp white shirt and a grey tie. There are people everywhere, all bearing sad faces and waiting for the funeral walk to the grave site to begin. Talk about feeling out of place, lost amid a bunch of people I do not know. I would probably leave discreetly if it wouldn't be for Christine, and how she needs support right now. Furthermore, grief engenders grief and my mere presence here is a painful reminder of my own losses.

I have never been so grateful for a tree as I am today, as the funeral plot is sheltered under a magnificent maple tree. I am standing under it right now and I do not intend to move an inch. Sweating like a pig would look uncool and undignified for this special occasion. I wonder how funeral parlor employees do it, dressed in black and carrying those heavy coffins during hot summer days. They all look stone-faced, relaxed and sweat-free. Special training at pallbearers' boot camp? I have to ask one someday.

All of a sudden, everyone stops talking and lines up on the

same side of the road, looking back at the funeral procession slowly approaching the grave site. Any such scene at any time would be touching and would incite deep feelings of respect, but the one I am witnessing at this moment is particularly difficult to bear as it involves the suffering of a person whose life has become very dear to me. As I watch her advance to her son's grave, I feel her pain and apprehension at the daunting task she's about to perform: burying the ashes of a person she loved more than herself, into a cold, dark and lonely hole in the ground.

What makes this disheartening scene even more agonizing is the fact that it is the second time around that life is playing a dark and cruel joke on Christine and her family. It's only ten years ago that cancer claimed the life of Tyson her middle son, an angel of a human being as I hear, inflicting a wound on her that has yet to be healed. It is by the side of Tyson's imposing funeral monument that Damon is to be entombed, and I can't even begin to understand how she and the rest of her family must feel. My heart truly goes out to them.

Everyone gathers around the burial site, speeches and anecdotes concerning the deceased are delivered, and all present at the scene do their best to keep their emotions in check. When the grand moment arrives, though, I am overwhelmed by the cloud of sadness that suddenly emanates from the crowd and I'm saddened as I watch Christine, dressed in a classy black dress, sobbing and shaking profusely as she lowers the urn into the hungry soil. She looks frail and the vulnerability she exudes renders her even more endearing to me. How I ache for her at this moment, how I long to rush to her side and hug her reassuringly to help soothe her pain. But that has yet to happen as I'm about to discover.

Funerals are always a bit daunting and depressing, but they are nevertheless the perfect occasion to express grief publicly and without judgement. It is therapeutic and necessary for many as it often marks the only time that they will allow themselves the liberty to express their feelings of loss. 'Get over it and get on with your life as soon as possible,' is most people's credo, which in my view is a mistake. There is no timeline for grieving, and everyone should be allowed to do so on their own terms. Unfortunately, the funeral ceremony is a dying tradition which I feel is perhaps due to the lack of understanding of its role and to the exorbitant expenses it brings about. Let's keep the tradition but alter its procedure I say.

When the ceremony is over and as the crowd is dispersing, Christine comes to talk with me to share her thoughts of the day. Not wanting to go into slippery territory as she is still very shaken up emotionally, I keep the conversation light and superficial. After chatting for a short while, we agree to meet at the local Canadian Legion pub in Alexandria for a drink in half an hour where a short celebration in honor of Damon is to take place. "Could you give a lift to my friend 'Tom' at the same time? He doesn't have his car and wants to come also," she asks. "Sure, it would be my pleasure," I reply and wave Tom over to ride back to town with me. Tom is an older gentleman, a woodworker, a poet, a fine man who I suspect has silently been a little taken by Christine's charms over the years. He's also a good talker and his engaging conversation keeps me good company all the way to Alexandria.

I stay at the pub for a short while, sipping a beer and trying to look as social as possible in that sea of strangers. Having had enough, I discreetly maneuver my way out of there. Christine gets a hold of me in the exit corridor and suggests that I come down to her apartment later on to spend some time together, have a bite and relax. 'Absolutely delighted!' I wanted to say, but in an effort to remain cool, I limited my enthusiastic *élan* to a reserved "Yes, I'll be glad to. What time do you want me there?" "Eight would be fine," she replies. "Great, I'll see you then," I say, and turn around and walk out the door, resisting the urge to risk a 'Fred Astaire' dance move.

I can't say the night goes as expected, as I don't have any expectations. My visit with Christine is mainly to support a friend going through a difficult period. But I have to admit that I also welcome any opportunity that allows me to be in her lovely company.

In one of our conversations, Christine told me that she loved to dance, and I came prepared to oblige. Rod Stewart's *Great American Song Book* is my choice and I am hoping that she will approve; "I love songs of the forties and fifties," she says enthusiastically. Great, I made a good choice, another point we have in common. I am also relieved to discover that her mood has elevated a couple of notches since I last saw her at the pub three hours ago. This tells me that I'm dealing with a person of character who doesn't let life beat her down. This is important to me as I have a lot of respect for people who handle adversity well.

We have a light snack: shrimp salad and white wine, and no dessert. Is this the secret to her gorgeous figure? I think and hope that maintaining such a diet in her company might help keep my slim silhouette intact also, a fact that is a priority for me. I have to say that I had more than a few brushes with the 'battle of the bulge' myself and I was teased, bullied, beaten up and laughed at for most of my youth. Heck, some of my, supposedly, friends even wrote songs to mock my pudginess. The desire to free myself from these tyrants and to overcome my struggle with the flab led me to get involved with nutrition, bodybuilding, boxing and martial arts and so on. Today my lean body is not due to faith, accident or genes, but to education, nutrition, diets, and restraints I impose on myself; otherwise, I would look like the Goodyear blimp.

What does all this stuff have to do with grieving? you may ask; and my answer is, a lot. It's a matter of attitude, of how we face the hardships of life. Whether it's fighting the fat bulge or the loss of a loved one, the dynamics are the same; we get hit, we fall down, we cry and whine a bit, we struggle to stand up, dust ourselves off and start again. "That's life," as Frank Sinatra would say. Nothing we do or say can ever change that.

Christine's behavior since the short time I've known her leads me to believe that she's the kind of person I would love to spend the rest of my life with. In spite of all the suffering she's been through (there's way more to her story than said here), she managed to remain an adorable, caring and loving human being and I lift my *chapeau* to her.

Content and satisfied with our meal, we sit down on her rather uncomfortable red velvety French antique settee and chat for hours. As we dance, the music of my buddy Rod is working its magic and Christine seems to enter into some kind of light trance and lets go of some of the day's tensions. "I had this pressure in my chest all day, and now as we dance, I can feel it go away. It's wonderful," she says. "You're an amazing dancer, Pierre." That comment makes my day or rather my night and I just want to slow dance with her forever, or at least for the rest of our little *soirée*.

That night before leaving, I pause at the door and risk a discreet kiss, well, not so discreet if you consider that I savor her delicious lips for way more than a few enjoyable seconds. "What are you doing to me?" she whispers with parted lips. "Just getting to know you better," I answer as I gently kiss her once more. With a silent sigh, I reluctantly leave her apartment, already longing for my next visit.

Fighting separation anxiety

The week that follows proves to be long and difficult as Christine is gone away to visit her sister for a week and I miss her a whole lot. The space she leaves is heavy and brings about all the pain and loneliness I experienced when Louise passed away. I carry a stubborn ache in the pit of my stomach, I have no appetite and I do not feel like seeing anyone even though I am lonely to the bone. I cannot help but recognize the sure signs of separation anxiety, as I recall my reaction when she informed me of her departure a week ago.

The huge emptiness that engulfed me when Louise died instantly reappeared when Christine broke the news to me on the phone. As I hung up the receiver, I immediately entered into panic mode at the thought of being alone once more, and if it would not have been for my pride, I'd have called back to pitifully plead with her not to go. How lame of me, a man who was always headstrong and independent. *It's just for a week, you moron, take a pill*, I scolded myself, but I just couldn't help it. It was like I was afraid she'd disappear, die or be abducted by aliens, never to be seen again. I was petrified of being left by myself and abandoned like that morning a year ago when I woke up in Louise's deathbed, alone in my empty living room. No matter how hard I tried, the emptiness followed me wherever I went and, breathing exercises or not, the hollowness I felt would just not go away...until I could speak with Christine again. It's amazing how fast one can become attached and dependent on another human being given the right circumstances. Grief is a troubling beast and can take you places you've never been before.

We had previously agreed to call each other every night around nine o'clock, and I would never have suspected that those magical moments would become so precious to me. Without fail, every time we talked, Christine's soothing voice would bring about a wonderful feeling of wellbeing that carried me through the night. Unfortunately though, the loneliness would rise up again like bubbles in a glass of soda the next morning and haunt me for hours until Christine's voice came to my rescue once more. That nightly phone call was rapidly becoming a crutch and I feared I had become dependent on it during that never-ending week. However, all is not lost and the whole episode helped open my eyes to the dangers and the unfairness of becoming too dependent on Christine.

Our relationship must not be based on dependency and

control, but on mutual respect and admiration. Nevertheless, overcoming the anxiety created by my separation from Christine poses a huge challenge for me and overcoming this anxiety will be a long and arduous journey I fear. Little did I know then that I would have numerous occasions to practice being separated from my lady as she is very active and likes to travel quite a bit.

Aside from that, nothing of importance happens and I drag my feet until she eventually comes back. During the following weeks, we see each other frequently, go out a lot and I feel whole again. I question if this is a good thing or not. Shouldn't I be whole by myself and not require another person's presence to complete me? Should I enter into a relationship based on these precepts or follow the concept by which mutual attraction and growth is based on the complementing of each other's needs? What should I do? Following my heart over my head has always been my way and I will do the same here again. I like where this kind of thinking led me and I trust that my inner wisdom will show me the way once more. Living each day the best I can and being true to myself is my guiding light. Learning to overcome my fears has always been my ultimate goal, and overcoming the challenges that a new relationship brings can only be beneficial for me.

October 9, 2011

My first visit to Christine's cottage; the idea of this book is born
"You want to come spend the weekend at my cottage?" Christine asks enthusiastically. "The weather will be nice and we could take advantage of the lake before I leave for France next week." Ouch, here we go again. My heart skips a beat. I can't help it; it's like a damn reflex now. My body gets instantly overwhelmed by a fear reaction just by hearing certain trigger words, sentences or innuendos that refer to departures, her departure mainly. Before I can even start to process her comments and reason with myself, I lose my composure. "Man oh man," I moan. I'm fried like an

egg in a hot pan. How the hell am I going to get rid of that crap? I take a deep breath and answer, "Yes, I would love it. It would be great."

The ride through the winding Quebec Gatineau Hills is fabulous and rapidly takes away my silly apprehensions of being left alone. *Let's enjoy my time with Christine and think no more of this foolishness,* I reason. But little did I know then, that I was about to find out how easy it would be to let go of my apprehension once we enter the route to Christine's cottage.

"I have to warn you that the roadway leading to my place is a little bumpy and challenging," says Christine as she lays on me a bunch of instructions on what I can expect along the way and how to proceed without destroying her car (she had asked me to take the wheel for the drive from Martintown, a test?). Anyway, after a back-breaking and brain-shattering ride that can only be compared to an off-road jeep run, we finally arrive at our destination, and I'm totally 'wowed.' The scene offered to me is out of this world and pulled directly from a 'country living' magazine cover and well worth the wild ride.

'Inspiring' is the only word I can use to describe the effect the place has on me. The cute two-story Swiss chalet, the welcoming dark brown rattan chairs and tables sitting on a large wooden deck, wrapping the house on two sides, the magnificent giant pine trees standing tall overlooking the lodge, the cozy private sandy beach alongside the typical cedar dock, all bring out the artist in me.

As I stand there in the midst of all this, trying to take in as much as I can of all this splendor, I am overwhelmed by the pungent scent of evergreens, and the wild flowers growing by the waterside. Magically I experience a sensation I thought I had lost forever: life, an unmistakable will to live, to create and to start a new beginning. Is it the strong energy of the place, Christine's presence in my space, getting reacquainted with past lives, memories, or my own ability to welcome a new life? I don't know and I don't care. What I do know, though, is that here and now I want to experience 'me' as a new man and embrace life to the fullest, whatever the cost. Opening up and letting go emotionally is definitely a very scary thing to do, but the rewards it offers are well worth the effort. Where will this exciting new adventure lead me? Time will tell.

During the day, Christine takes me for a visit of the surrounding area, enlightens me on the history of the place, introduces me to her uncle, aunt and cousins who live nearby, and we spend the rest of the day chatting non-stop like two teenagers on a camping trip with nothing else to do. Knowing that the place had no electricity, I came prepared and I had brought my battery-operated CD player so we could relax and have a few dances to the soothing sound of our favorite 'crooners.'

I do believe I talked about unforgettable times before, and the following 'Hollywood moment' will forever have a special place in my heart.

Darkness has fallen upon us, we have just finished our delicious meal and are polishing up a bottle of sumptuous French Pinot Noir wine when, suddenly, Tony Bennett's soothing voice breaks through the air with his melodic rendition of 'The Way You Look Tonight.' Surrendering to the entrancing music, I stand and ask *ma belle* to join me for a dance on the patio.

I could not have planned this moment any better, even if I'd wanted to: standing on the deck embracing each other softly, we give in to the sexy rhythm of the melody as we slow dance cheek to cheek, the star-riddled sky shows off a bright silvery moon, and a soothing warm southerly breeze caresses our heated bodies. Our intertwined beings get lost in the magic of the moment, nothing else exists, and I fall in Love.

The next day, even though I'm walking on a cloud, I'm a little apprehensive and I do not look forward to leaving this haven for our trip back to town. I dread what's going to happen when we'll be back home: dropping Christine off at her apartment and driving off to my empty house. Bummer, I already feel the pangs of loneliness pricking at me just thinking about it. *Dammit, don't let this ruin the rest of what could be a beautiful day with her. Shake yourself off, man. Today is the only time you've got left with her; after that she's gone for two weeks. Better make the best of it.*

Two whole weeks, geez, it's like an eternity. I start to freak out at the mere thought of it, and the more I try to calm down, the worst my uneasiness gets.

I take a deep breath in an effort to clear my mind and I focus strictly on one thing, enjoying the rest of my time with Christine.

The following days, I somehow succeed in keeping my mind occupied by puttering around the house. Eventually though, the dreadful day arrives and I take off to pick up Christine and drive her to the Ottawa airport as planned.

Her flight is late at night and, as required, we arrive three hours ahead, which gives us enough time to hang around and chat. My inner battle is worse than ever and I must make constant efforts to control a mounting nausea as the time of her departure approaches. I do my best to look amicable and happy, but inwardly I stupidly hope that she will change her mind at the last minute and decide not to go to France and stay with me. Dream on, buddy. Her trip has been planned for months; why would she do that now? You're not that important to her yet. And as my deliberations go on and on, I hear a disembodied voice say: "All passengers to flight...to Paris via Toronto please proceed to gate..." and my heart skips a beat. Here we go.

With finality, I look at Christine's eyes for the last time as I kiss her goodbye and, with a heavy heart, I watch her leave to go to line up at the gate. As she waits, she regularly looks back at me, smiles and warms my heart with a discreet wave of the hand. But the elation doesn't last and the dread returns with a vengeance the moment I look ahead at the departure gate. Eventually she gets there though, and my heart sinks when I see her wave one last time, blow me a kiss and disappear into the dark beyond my reach. I hate goodbyes; they always give me 'the mush' and today is worse than ever.

Not wanting to fret too much on what had just happened, I rapidly spin around, and walk back to my car; once ensconced for the drive home, I turn the radio on for company. I need to hear a voice right now, and drive back home to my little house which seems emptier than ever.

Back to your breathing exercises, man, right now; fight this, there's no other choice. Go take a walk along the river, go to the gym and work out until you drop. Finally as time goes by, my strategies work. I manage to take a hold of myself, and my life returns to some kind of normalcy. *Being alone for two weeks will be a good occasion for me to work on this damn separation anxiety thing*, I think, ready for a fight. Plus I have this three-day workshop on mental energies coming up next weekend; that'll keep me occupied for a while. But little did I know that my separation anxiety problem was nothing compared to the brutal storm that was about to be dumped on me.

The missed phone calls—grief engendering grief
Present
It's one of those new fancy cell phones and I have been holding it in my hands part of the day for fear of missing her call. Christine is vacationing in France right now and, as planned, I'm attending a seminar at the Spiritual Science Fellowship's head office in Montreal. In order not to disturb the workshop leader and the participants, I have silenced the ringer and set the phone on vibrate only. She has been gone for a week and I have barely had any news from her. I miss her a whole lot and I'm very eager to be comforted by the sound of her lovely voice. Our original plan was that on that particular day, she would try to call me whenever she could find a darn phone, a dubious task to achieve from the backwoods of the South of France, where she is visiting

old chateaux. This part of the country may be beautiful, but it is also very bereft of hi-tech communication devices.

So when break time finally arrives, and wondering why I have not heard from her yet, I anxiously check my phone more closely and notice a small blue light flashing on the screen announcing that I have a voice message. Bang, a rush of blood instantly flushes my face, a painful stab hits me right in the chest and, with unbelievable disappointment, I realize that she had managed to find a phone, she had called me and I had missed her call.

June 22, 1985

Past

It was 11 p.m. and I was dreaming of the incessant irritating ring of a telephone, when I realized that it is in fact my own phone that is ringing. So, forcing myself out of the deep sleep I was in, I stumbled around awkwardly in an effort to shut the darn thing up as soon as possible, but unfortunately I wasn't quick enough and the phone dropped dead silent before I could pick it up.

You see, due to the magic of modern technology, I was in the habit of transferring my home phone line to my office, so I wouldn't miss any personal calls during the day. At night when I came back, I reversed the process so I could answer my calls from home. But for some reason, that night I had forgotten to do the procedure and the line was automatically transferred to my office where he had left a message. A painful reminder of my mistake. Little did I know at the time that this omission would have dramatic consequences on my life for years to come.

I will always remember that devastating Sunday morning, the knock on my front door and the young soldier holding his kepi under his arm, all dressed up in his formal army uniform, saying with a shaking voice: "Mr Milot, I regret to inform you that your son, Steve, has passed away."

Shock and disbelief cannot even come close to describing what I felt. It was like being hit in the forehead with a baseball bat. I very nearly fainted onto my couch, too stunned to even cry.

Steve, my beautiful and gentle son, was a soldier in the Canadian Army and at the time was in special training at the Suffield training camp in Alberta. He was in the routine of calling me every night to chat, but due to the set of unfortunate dramatic circumstances that occurred that night, he was gone forever, taken away from me, and I had missed his call.

Present; back at the seminar

Abnormally perturbed and destabilized by my cell phone incident, I have to leave the seminar early. I'm disturbed and fidgety to the point of not being able to stand in one place. With a horrible feeling of dread stirring up in my gut, I hurriedly walk to my car to head back home. As I drive I can feel a menacing storm brewing up inside, which is not entirely a new phenomenon for me, I might add. In fact, I have had these troubling grieving episodes regularly since I became a widower, but I can tell that this time this one is going to be a doozy and that I'm in for a wild ride.

As the miles fade away, I can feel the downpour approaching and I'm confused as to the nature of my discombobulation. I naturally assume that my emotional discomfort has something to do with the bitter disappointment I feel at missing Christine's phone call, but there's something else and it puzzles me. I have known Christine for such a short while, why do I react so strongly? Why does the intensity of my feelings seem so terribly out of proportion? The whole situation bothers me so much that I even doubt my decision to enter into a new romantic affair at this stage in my life.

Do I want to set myself up for the risks and challenges of adjusting to a new relationship and everything that it involves? After going through so much pain and sorrow when Louise passed away, do I want to run the risk of going through the same thing again? Will Christine be sick too? Will I be sick and impose this on her? Did I take the leap too quickly? So many questions to which I have no answers, but the digging through my very core is having its effects. Ultimately I'm emotionally overwhelmed and the cleansing tears appear and soon roll down my cheeks abundantly.

As far as my new relationship with Christine is concerned, the only thing I know for sure is that I am happier since I've met her and that everything in my life is more beautiful when she's with me. My life has meaning once more and offers so many new possibilities. I had lost all of this in the hollowness of widowhood. Yes, I conclude after some clarity has come through, it's worth sticking my head out. The enjoyment I feel being with her far outweighs the risks of reliving something that may never come anyway. I always followed my heart before and I am glad I'm doing it again.

In time though, after the bizarre mixture of tears of joy and sorrow has cleared some of the confusion, I realize that the real pain hasn't arrived yet. This is just a transition, the boost I needed to struggle and dig my way in deeper into my repressed past. I am dreadfully afraid that the real issue of my disconcerted state has yet to come.

As I progress through my trials and tribulations, faded images of my son start to appear, and with a sorrowful aching heart, I realize how deeply I miss him. I thought I had made my peace with his loss, but apparently not. As the ride home painfully goes on, I am flooded with memories that I had kept locked away securely for 27 years. Imagine, 27 years of guilt for not having de-transferred that stupid phone line and missing his call. Oh man, so much pain. I am so overwhelmed by the immensity of it all that I almost suffocate. I cannot help but obsessively think that if I would have picked up his call that night, I might have dissuaded him from taking his friend's place at touring the army base with the service jeep, thus the accident might not have happened and he could still be alive.

I visualize him in a future that will never be, walking happily through my front door with his wife and kids and saying in his usual manner that I loved so much, "Hi Dad, how are you today?" I can imagine my big guy hugging me with his strong arms when Louise died, saying, "It's OK to cry, Dad. I love you," and affectionately bringing me solace when I need it most. But it is not to be and life apparently has other plans for both of us. *Oh vengeful gods, why are ye so selfish and take back our loved ones so young?* I think in anguish. Guilt is such a resilient emotion and hard to disconnect from.

Once home, I get myself a stiff drink and crash on my leather couch and continue crying my eyeballs out until my lachrymatory glands beg for mercy. The whole experience is an eye-opener for me as it proves one more time that grief needs to be expressed sooner or later, and that anyone who prides themselves in having successfully managed to tuck it away in some confined corner of their mind is sadly mistaken. Eventually, triggered by some kind of life event or by the sufferings of another loss, grief will sneak back on you at some point and often at the most inconvenient of times too. If it's true that 'the truth will set you free,' expressing your grief, even years later, will also set you free. It took me 27 years to finally let go of the repressed sufferings of losing my son. It crept back on me at a very vulnerable moment and it very nearly crushed me.

Many days later, as I reflect back on that dreadful day, I sense that a weight has been lifted from me and that the pain has eased off quite a bit. Will my soul ever find peace again though? My heart says yes, and with time, if I continue to let go, the healing will surely set in.

All that because of a couple of missed phone calls.

The two weeks finally end and my baby is coming back home. The time alone has taught me a lot and was a real crash course in learning how to negotiate the slippery emotional hill of separation anxiety. I was reacquainted with the reality that under the right set of circumstances, even the strongest of us can be brought down emotionally and shredded to pieces in a heartbeat.

As I see Christine walking through the arrival gate at the airport, my joy returns and I feel reconnected and alive again. I realize sadly, though, that my battle against separation anxiety is far from over. It's one thing to be happy for the return of my loved one after a short separation, but it's worrisome to think that I was so miserable in her absence. The line is fine between missing someone and putting your life on hold and entertaining a constant sense of dread until that person returns. I'll have to work hard on that one. Dammit, there's always something more to learn and overcome, isn't there? Even though I'm happy with Christine, I feel that life is a constant uphill battle.

The following weeks are good and I do not get too many opportunities to work on my little problem as we are constantly together and enjoying life. We close the cottage for the winter, we have a party at my house where Christine introduces me to her many friends, and we fly to Freeport to cool our heels in the sun for Christmas.

Year 2012

All good things come to him who waits

The year starts well and I hope it's a sign of good things to come. Not long after our return from Freeport, we go right back out to Florida for two weeks. There's a twist to this in the sense that Christine, previous to meeting me, had arranged to visit her friend in Madeira Beach and she was held to that promise. So she flew in the first week as arranged and we decided that I was to drive there to meet with her and spend the rest of the week in a cottage I rented for that occasion. *A little practice for me,* I think, as I say goodbye to her at the gate before her flight takes off. But practice makes perfect and I find that I'm not as discombobulated as when she left for France. Way to go, Pierre, making progress here.

En route back home from Florida, we make a detour and fly into Toronto so that I can meet Susan, Christine's younger sister, and her mother, who lives in a retirement home near Susan's. We have a nice time there until things take a turn for the worse when Christine suffers a bad fall at Susan's place and injures her back seriously enough to warrant a trip to the hospital in an ambulance.

"No broken bones, but a hairline fracture in one of your vertebrae," says the attending doctor. "Nothing else to do but rest and painkillers," and he hands her a prescription. We scoop out of there for the trip to Susan's house where we stay another couple of days before driving five hours back to my house. What is a misfortune for Christine is in a way a bonus for me as she is bed-ridden and needs assistance, which I'm more than glad to provide. The days and weeks go by and we feel so at ease with each other in the same house that we decide she will move in officially.

February 14

A decisive date

We have a nice St Valentine's Day dinner to celebrate our decision and finalize the details of her move. The day is a double whammy as it marks my return to the music world as a singer and keyboardist. We were having our dinner at The Georgian House Restaurant in Alexandria which is owned by a friend of Christine's. After some discussion with him, it is agreed that I will show up and entertain with my Hammond organ and keyboard every Friday night in the main dining room. If you would have told me a year ago that I would get a second round as a professional musician, I would have rolled on the floor laughing as I was certain that that part of my life was over and done with. It took Christine's presence and the joy she brings in my new life to reawaken the artist in me.

More practice in my struggle to overcome separation anxiety

when I decide to fly to Seattle to further my training as a therapeutic counselor. This time it is me that is leaving, hence crossing the gate at the airport is a little easier. Nevertheless, when I open the door to my lonely hotel room in Seattle, a whiff of oppression invades me and I start to suffocate. God, I hate hotel rooms when I'm alone, and now I miss Christine acutely. I reach to open the window but it's sealed shut. Damn it. I initiate a series of cleansing breaths to regain some kind of control. *Wow, what a therapist you make. You need a therapist, more than becoming a therapist yourself.* I'm disgusted with my reaction. But soon, the effect of my efforts pays off and I eventually calm down. Tomorrow will be a busy day and I won't have time to fuss around with this nonsense. And I reach for the assistance of my buddy Mr Scotch and dial my phone number to reach Christine at home.

The following days in training pass quickly, and my return at the hotel each night becomes a little bit less dramatic. The time of my departure finally arrives and with my brand-new certificate safely tucked up in my briefcase I cannot be happier to get back home.

A week after my return, Christine and I decide to complete another training, this time a palliative care course for caregivers at the Cornwall Hospice, a move which will definitely add a few more stripes to my résumé. This was an initiative I would never have taken by myself. Thanks to Christine's influence and a lot of work on my part, I am becoming a pretty solid individual, a far cry from who I was a year ago.

April 21

The Big Day

This is it, folks, my baby's moving in with me and I couldn't be happier. In anticipation of this, I got rid of my old furniture which was dated anyway and a painful reminder of a previous life that I left behind. If I'm going to have a new start, I may as well go all the way. Christine is a little embarrassed that I go to such extents to make room for her stuff. Life is for the living, I remind her. "If I welcome you into my house it is with open arms and I want you to feel right at home. Bring your stuff, honey, it'll just be a new decorating challenge for me"…and it was.

Christine is a world traveler and has gathered a rather eclectic collection of objects, unusual gizmos, artworks and not-your-everyday type of furniture, I might say. Luckily she has a predilection for the French culture and, as I have already mentioned to you, I am a Canadian of French descent and love everything that is French (particularly the women with their cute little accent, but I didn't say that to Christine…yet).

What an exhausting day it was! Well, not for me actually, as, aside from walking around with a screwdriver in my hand and a strained grimace on my sweaty face making me look busy, I didn't lift a single finger that day. (Being an old fart with a bad back has its privileges, you know.) The others, Brandon, Christine's son, and his friends, did the hard lifting and carrying. When we think of antique furniture, we think of wood, thick, solid and heavy, very heavy, and Christine's antique couch, beds, armoires were all that and even more. Man, my heart goes to those poor buggers as I see them breaking their backs and sweating bullets as they grunt their way from the truck to the house and up the stairs to the second floor with a massive oak English secretary and struggle to make it fit into the room that is to become Christine's study. Man, I'm tired just looking at them.

"We're proud of you kids," Christine and I say. While sipping a well-deserved cold brew, they all chant in unison: "Yeah, yeah, our pleasure," as they exhibit big smiles. Flat out and glad the move is over, they are eager to open the little white cash-filled envelopes that Christine hands them for their services.

Now the fun part starts as we redecorate the house. The exotic and eclectic mix of Christine's French antique furniture and my art pieces and musical instruments gives my little Victorian country house an absolutely adorable look, worthy of the cover picture of a 'country chic' decoration magazine.

Life's good today and I can barely feel the scars of my losses. I'm at the top of the cresting wave now and I do my best to fight off the thought that it could come crashing down on me at any moment. I have experienced the brutal roller-coaster ride of grief many times before and this makes it hard for me to enjoy the moment. Nevertheless, I must stand strong and follow my own advice. 'Tomorrow I will take care of tomorrow; today I take care of today.' I smile as I look into Christine's beautiful blue eyes and I count my blessings.

My new life with Christine is fantastic and full of joy, but it feels a little weird to have another woman in my house. What does Louise think of that from where she is? How does it feel to Christine to roam the same corridors that Louise did, to use the same bathroom, sit in the living room where Louise died, and sleep in the same bed as Louise and I slept? The bed is one of the few pieces of furniture we decided to keep. Although Christine never talks about it and seems to integrate very well, I'm sure that at times she has her moments. What a brave girl!

Time to say farewell to Max

I've been thinking about it for a while now. Heck, I've been thinking about it since Louise passed away, but I just couldn't do it. For heaven's sake, what gives me the right to decide on when or where a life should end and make the final call to say: "It's time"? How horribly painful and devastating it is for me to decide to go ahead and kill a faithful friend who shared my everyday life through thick and thin, who has lovingly put up with my idiosyncrasies and bad moods for years without a simple complaint.

How can I look into Max's tired eyes and tell him, "Time to go, buddy," pick him up because he's too tired to walk, and carry him to his final voyage? How can I stand to hold him on the vet's doomsday table while he makes the fatal injection? How can I stay alone in that room with him as he lies there in deathly immobility and gently pat his soft black fur and kiss him my last farewell? How can I stand the horrible feeling of sadness that overwhelms my entire being while I walk out of the vet's office with teary eyes, holding on tightly to Christine's hand?

I did it because it was my duty to a friend who was counting on me to have the wisdom to recognize when it was time to end his sufferings and the courage to do the necessary, and I stood up to the task. Now, I like to think that he's enjoying peace and comfort curled up for eternity on Louise's lap. What a great image for me to hold on to. Farewell, my faithful friend, Xxx

Back at the cottage and the start of this book

"You should write a book on your story," people keep telling me. "How you put your life aside to become Louise's sole caretaker 24 hours per day, seven days a week for three years without failing or getting sick yourself." Many people wanted to know how I survived the debilitating roller-coaster ride of hope and despair and how I managed to come out the other end in one piece. They said it would be an encouragement to others walking down the same path to hear my story. But every time, I rejected the idea. I said that it would be too painful. I explained that I have to think about it, I'm not ready yet. I'll know when I'm ready. They were lame excuses but the truth is that the thought of doing it lingered in my mind…Maybe…Someday…

The ride to the cottage that Friday morning is awesome. Christine is driving of course. "I like driving," she says casually as some sort of justification. "Plus it gives you a chance to enjoy the scenery, don't you think?" But I have a sneaky suspicion that there is something more to this. As I will soon find out, Christine is the best backseat driver I've ever met and that she'll soon have me begging for mercy with her constant: "red light ahead, brake, brake, you're too close to the middle line, you're too close to the shoulder, you're going too fast, too slow," etc. So, short of duck-taping her mouth or wearing ear plugs, I now let her be the captain of the show, ride slingshot, kick my shoes off, stretch and rest my legs on the dashboard and relax.

After surviving the ride on the bumpy trail that leads from the main road to the cottage, we finally arrive at Christine's humble abode, park the jeep, and, the minute I set foot on the ground, I am in awe again, like last year. I'm overwhelmed by the pungent scent of evergreen trees and fresh clean mountain air. The sight that's offered to my eyes is spectacular: the Swiss cottage surrounded by the large wooden deck, the sandy beach at arm's reach, the large pine trees and the weeds growing amid the rocky shore on the other side of the cedar dock are to die for.

Nothing has changed, it seems, since we last were here. It's as if time stood still during the winter and started again in the spring. I think, *What a beautiful and charming place.* At that moment I understand very well why Christine loves it so much; it's so inspiring, could this be it for me…maybe…I'll see.

It takes us a mere two hours to settle in, eat and sit by the fireplace and enjoy a glass of fine wine. *What a life,* I think, and as we sit on the same couch as we did a year ago, I cannot help but remember with tenderness the night Christine and I shared a slow dance on the deck by the moonlight and how I'm in love with her more than ever.

The next morning, without preamble, I get up, get myself a cup of hot java, grab my computer, kiss Christine, climb up the stairs to the second-floor terrace, sit at the cute patio table and start typing: It's ten o'clock in the morning and I just finished my first cup of coffee…

The End

Epilogue

Putting together this piece has been for me a real catharsis and proved itself at times to be an excruciating emotional exercise. I have undergone many transformations since I started writing this book three years ago. More than once, I wished I'd never started it. But I could not stop myself, I could not let it go; it was like a drug and I was hooked. I often thought that no matter how long it will take, this book will see the light.

The intensity of my grief at times was such that I had to take breaks from writing in order to breathe and recover from the emotional upheaval that was mercilessly pounding my inner core. The digging into my painful past was taking me through an emotional roller-coaster ride of sadness, anger, resentment and fear that was burying my normally cool and easy-going nature. I was afraid that through my wild mood changes, I would push away the very same loved ones I wanted and needed the most.

I was not a picnic to live with and I have to praise Christine, my angel, for having stuck with me through those years. She must have seen something in me that I didn't yet. I thank her so much for that and I'm sure that if it would not have been for her loving presence, courage, understanding and inspiration, I would not have completed this journey and finished my project.

It was well worth the effort, though, as, in retrospect, when I reread my text, I notice the subtle changes that took place in me over the years. The initial sadness and overall feeling of emptiness that was my everyday companion has phased out quite a bit, if not totally. The original anger, bitterness and resentment that was plaguing me daily has also taken a back seat to more happiness and cheerfulness. I smile and laugh much more now. My drinking has toned down dramatically also, although I still enjoy my favorite distilled brew in a more civilized manner. Thanks to Christine's influence, I have increased my socializing skills considerably and my tendency to cement myself in reclusiveness has taken a step down.

I've even managed to take a grip on separation anxiety, the most sneaky and tenacious invader I've ever known. It showed its ugly head sometime after I met Christine. Only recently can I claim to have some kind of control over the crushing fear of losing another loved one, of losing Christine. This, I anguished, could possibly set me back years and throw me into the devastating grips of torment once more.

I feel I'm pretty much out of the woods now. But will I ever heal completely? Will I ever get rid of that underlying feeling of sadness that still plagues me once in a while? 'Time heals all wounds,' they say, and I believe I'm winning the battle.

If the passing of Louise was the most devastating event in my life, finding Christine because of this loss becomes a welcomed mitigating circumstance that helps me keep things in perspective: without losing Louise, I would never have met Christine.

I am not a religious man, but I'm nevertheless open to the concept of an afterlife, whatever it may be. As a hopeless romantic and a dreamer, I like to give in to the idea that Louise from the spirit world was instrumental in pulling some strings so that Christine and I could meet and become 'a match made in Heaven.'

Life goes on and I count my blessings every day. If I look back from where I came from to where I am now, I can say that I am pleased with my accomplishments. I have learned and matured of my own accord and I took on successfully life's unwarranted challenges.

'A wounded dear leaps highest.' (Emily Dickinson)

Appendix I: Defining Grief

Grieving Process

Grief is painful and at times the pain seems unbearable. It is a period when mixed emotions come and go, often without warning. How long this difficult period lasts depends on the relationship with the deceased, the circumstances of the death and the situation of the survivors. There is no precise timeline for the grieving period; it can last weeks, months and even years, but one thing is certain: it eases over time. In order to escape, some people may be tempted to deny the pain. But studies show that denial does not help to get over the loss in the long run. Repressed painful emotions can turn up in unrecognized and destructive ways. *Understanding the emotions of grief, its feelings and symptoms is an important step in healing and in helping other grievers.* According to experts, when grieving is done properly there is growth and maturity.

Different Types of Grief

There are four major types of grief: anticipatory, traumatic, disenfranchised, and unresolved or complicated.

Anticipatory Grief

Refers to grieving before the actual loss has occurred.

- The process allows individuals the time to absorb the reality of loss in a gradual fashion
- The individual or the family progressively begins the task of mourning which happens naturally; it is a subconscious process
- It often allows the survivor to go on more quickly after the loss has occurred

Emotions a person may experience during anticipatory grief:

- *sadness* at the thought of the impending death of the loved one and of their plans that will go unfulfilled
- *frustration* from the survivor due to his/her own inability to accept the coming death of the loved one
- *guilt* from the survivor concerning things that he/she may have said to the dying person
- *anger* from the survivor towards the doctor for not being able to do more for the dying person
- *anger* towards the sick person for not trying hard enough to heal him/herself
- *anger* against God for allowing this
- *loneliness* caused by the fact that the sick person is no longer an active part of their everyday life
- *hope* that the sick person will recover, and dread that he/she will become sick again; a veritable exhausting roller-coaster ride

The survivor may find strength in his/her spirituality or own life experience.

Traumatic Grief

Occurs when a death is

- sudden, unexpected and/or violent
- caused by the action of another person, an accident, a suicide, homicide or other catastrophic event
- from natural causes without any history of illness

Situations or emotions a person may face during traumatic grief:

- shatters the world of the survivor

- searches for answers and confronting the unfairness of life
- feelings of helplessness in the face of a situation a person cannot control
- factors which may compound grief: death is unconfirmed, physical body not found, etc.

After the initial protective numbness of the early stages of grief is gone, pain of the loss may become real and return in full force.

Disenfranchised Grief
The result of a loss for which an individual does not have a socially recognized right, role or capacity to grieve.

Defining disenfranchised grief
The relationship between two individuals is not socially recognized:

- gays
- May/September relationships
- the loss of an adult sibling
- the loss is not a person: the loss of a job, an object, a dear pet, a separation/divorce, youth, beauty, etc.
- the relationship was not approved by the family: cultural or religious differences
- the way the person died is not as appropriate as other causes of deaths
- the griever is not grieving as people would expect
- the griever is not socially recognized

Complicated/Unresolved Grief
Grief and mourning become prolonged. The griever is stuck and may become dysfunctional.

Symptoms of complicated grief:

- suicidal thoughts/plans
- self-destructive behavior
- major sleep and eating disturbances
- continued and increasing outbursts of rage with violent implications
- radical sudden shocking changes in lifestyle
- constant feelings of emptiness and meaninglessness
- extreme rage and bitterness over the loss
- constantly searching for the lost loved one in familiar places
- tenacious denial of death and sense of disbelief
- intense longing and yearning for the deceased

Major Types of Losses

Loss of a spouse/partner

Losing a spouse may be one of the most traumatic and destabilizing of all losses, even if it is anticipated. It can be overwhelming as it encompasses so many changes forced upon the survivor: loss of a daily presence, identity, financial partner, shared household tasks, etc. The longer you live with someone, the more you and your spouse learn to adapt, depend and respond to each other's values and perceptions. This is especially true when two people 'grow up' together in the relationship. When one partner is gone, there is no more identity as a couple, there is no 'us' or 'we' anymore, only 'I', 'me alone'. The loneliness can be shattering and the personal and social identity must be rebuilt.

Loss of a child

They say that when you lose a spouse you lose your present, when you lose a parent you lose your past, and that when you lose a child you lose your future and this can be very discouraging for a parent. The grief experienced by the loss of a son or daughter is intense and prolonged. It is not in the natural order of things and parents do not expect to outlive their children. The child is biologically and emotionally a part of the parents, and when the death occurs, they feel that part of them has died also. The role of nurturer is also lost in the process. Parents lose their future grandchildren or may lose contact with existing grandchildren. These losses add to the grief of parents, and their faith/belief system is often affected.

Loss of a parent

When death comes to a loved one, it is always too soon. Whatever age we may be, the finality of losing a parent is often a traumatic life experience. There is always some kind of regret for not speaking the important words: I love you, thank you, I'm sorry, I forgive you. As we grow through adulthood, there is still that inner security of having one among us who has journeyed through life's trials that we have not yet faced. Losing our parents through our maturing years robs us of this feeling of security.

Loss of an adult/teenage sibling

When adults/teenagers lose a sibling, they often feel abandoned by society, causing their grief to be disenfranchised. The attention and sympathy goes mostly to the parents. Brothers' and sisters' grief remains unrecognized and they are expected to 'get over it' quickly. If they do not, they are encouraged to feel guilty for grieving too long.

When someone has been a part of your life since birth, your identity is based on having them around. They make up part of the unbroken wholeness that defines who you are. Because each sibling is different in character, they help to support each other by these same differences. By doing so, siblings actually loan each other their strengths, and when one of the siblings dies, that strength is lost, and the survivor's identity with it. It takes time to rebuild a life and to grow within you the parts once carried by your brothers or sisters. You don't 'get over it' as much as you 'grow through it'.

Children's understanding of death

Children understand death very differently than adults do. Their perception of death varies according to their developmental stage. All children develop at different rates and it is very important that parents learn to identify the different stages in order to deal with them appropriately.

Newborn to three years

At that stage there is no understanding of death. The infant absorbs emotions of others around him/her and can sense when there is excitement, sadness, anxiety in the home and they know intuitively when a significant person is missing. The toddler may exhibit changes in eating and nursing patterns.

Three to six years

Child thinks death is reversible and temporary like going to sleep or like when a parent goes to work or on a visit. Child believes that people who die will come back. Through some kind of 'magical thinking', he/she believes their thoughts, actions, words caused the death and that they can bring back the deceased. At that stage they are still greatly impacted by the parent's emotional state.

Six to nine years

Child begins to understand the finality of death. He/she sees death as a taker or a spirit that comes and 'gets you'; fears that death is contagious and that other loved ones will 'catch it' too; tends to connect death with violence and may ask "Who killed him?", continues to have difficulty expressing feelings verbally, but begins asking concrete questions; may suffer from increased aggression.

Nine to thirteen years

Child's understanding of death is nearer adult's understanding of death; more aware of the finality of death and the impact that death has on them. Concerned with how their world will change with the loss of a relationship; reluctant to open up and may have delayed grief reactions. They enter into a fragile independence stage and begin to develop an interest in rituals and how spirituality affects lives.

Thirteen to eighteen years

The adolescent has an adult understanding of death. Death is viewed as an interruption and is the enemy. May intellectualize and romanticize death. May act indifferently to the death of someone close as a protection against feelings. May need permission to grieve and may want to grieve with his/her peers, not adults. May have suicidal thoughts and difficulty with long-term planning. Questions his/her religious beliefs.

The loss to suicide

Recovery from the suicide of someone close is a monumental task, as suicide leaves deep scars on the survivor. The process of healing a broken heart from a loss by suicide is a slow and painful journey. Survivors have to learn to live with unanswered questions and acknowledge their feelings of anger. They may feel robbed of pleasant memories as they are haunted by the replay of the details surrounding the final event. They have to allow time for the bad memories to dissipate before they can access the good memories. They have to learn to turn guilt into forgiveness, accept the loneliness and rebuild their self-esteem.

Those who have experienced the suicide of a loved one have

to 'take heart' and learn to let go of blaming themselves or the deceased for their unhappiness.

Other Important Losses

Even though not deemed as important as the loss of a loved one by death, a number of other losses can warrant many of the emotions and symptoms described earlier.

Losing a life partner to separation or divorce may be demoralizing and destabilizing and, depending on the closeness of the relationship, be as devastating as a loss by death.

Losing a faithful pet who shared your life for years may be devastating and leave an enormous empty space.

Losing a job may have important repercussions on one's daily life and require some period of grieving and adjustment.

In essence, all kinds of loss require grieving. Loss engenders grieving and all feelings of grief should be taken seriously. Emotions generated by grief should always be dealt with as soon as possible.

The Key Concepts of Grief

According to J. Shep Jeffreys, author of *Helping Grieving People: When Tears Are Not Enough*:

Grief is a universal phenomenon (with cultural differences) among human beings.

It is a reaction to loss, that is, the breaking of an attachment bond that is common to all people. No matter what race, gender, color or creed, the similarity of anguished faces of loss is apparent, and the wailing lament of a person losing a loved one looks and sounds the same everywhere.

Grief comes from both tangible and intangible losses.

Grief is not always a response to death as most would think. Many other faces of loss can trigger a grief reaction. Loss is experienced when anything that we have become attached to is gone.

Grief is a natural reflex that exists to enhance survival.
At a primitive level, the human organism acts to connect with those upon whom it depends for survival. When this connection is not possible, the reaction is grief. The human grief response contains within it the basic drive to restore the attachment to the lost object. When reattachment is not possible, the individual may exhibit despair and associated mourning behaviors such as crying, sighing, withdrawal, depression or become disorganized.

Grief is generally an adaptive response, although it may be characterized by temporary disruptions in life.
The grief reaction presents a departure from normal life functioning and may be considered by some as a form of maladaption; crying, raging, etc. However, in the same way the physical body needing time to heal itself would enter into a phase of reduced activity, the psychological wound of loss requires a similar period of being 'out of commission with life' for a while in order to recuperate.

Grief is a natural phenomenon, although complications and illness can develop from it.
Natural grieving can go wrong and severely limit life activities when levels of depression, anxiety, rage and guilt become extreme and prolonged. When that happens, the grieving person is at risk of physical and emotional illness and therapy should be sought.

Grieving is complex and dynamic and varies between individuals and among cultures.
Grief is complex and as such may manifest as physical pain and discomfort, as intellectual and emotional distress, as social

dysfunction and spiritual discontinuity. Grief is dynamic because it changes morning to night time, from day to day, or from week to week.

The complexities of an individual's grief are also influenced by the ethnic and cultural traditions associated with death and loss.

Avoidance and denial are typical ways people soften or keep out the reality of painful loss.

Denial is an important stage in the grieving process and I will expand on that later on. But for now, let's just say that denial enables us to take the harsh reality of loss in small doses. This is a normal and very human characteristic that enables us to go on with living. Some people describe this as feeling numb.

Grief/Mourning Defined

The term 'grief' may be used in a variety of ways, e.g. to describe the behavior seen when people are mourning a death (dressing in black, etc.) or to indicate that a person is having a hard time getting over a loss (overwhelmed by emotions).

Common Myths

According to Jeffreys, there are several myths that people may fall back on when coping with loss or the threat of loss.

They are:

- "I can handle this on my own."
- "I don't need to talk about it."
- "They can't know how I feel."
- "My pain, anger and fear will just go away by itself."
- "Bad things also happen to other people."
- "If I don't think about it, it's as if nothing has happened or will happen."

The first four myths are examples of the human impulse to bend reality and hold off the pain anyway that we can. The last two myths are examples of keeping bad news at arm's length to prevent us from experiencing pain. Making use of these myths is a form of denial (defense mechanism) and is very normal.

Denial and Avoidance: useful shock absorbers

Denial is often perceived as running away from reality. A grieving person who finds the need to escape from the harsh reality of loss is often criticized as being weak and lacking the strength of character to face the painful truth of what has happened. However, denial acts as a very efficient protection against pain unless it becomes permanent, creates medical problems or renders a person dysfunctional. Denial and avoidance allow us to absorb the horrible reality a bit at a time.

In some cases, denial can be used to avoid grieving people, which is very typical and understandable, and people who act this way are not necessarily 'bad'. Contact with grieving people can eat away at our own emotional energy and denial system. Avoiding them shelters us from our own hidden emotional baggage which we are not ready to let go of yet.

The Seven Principles of Human Grief (Jeffreys)

1. You cannot fix or cure grief.
Grief is normal; it is not an illness that needs to be cured. The grief reaction is a combination of thoughts, physical and emotional feelings, and behaviors that enable us to survive. We cannot go over, around or under grief; we have to go through it. Being a non-judgmental and patient listener is the best way to help a grieving person sail along.

2. There is no one right way to grieve.
Everybody grieves differently and this must be respected. Each

culture has its own norms about how grief is expressed. Grief reactions also depend upon one's family, personality and gender, e.g. men don't cry, women cry, older adults contain their grief, etc.

3. There is no universal timetable for the grief journey.
How long does it take to go through grief? How long does it take before we feel normal again?

We don't heal on anyone else's schedule but our own and it will take as long as it takes to rise from the ashes of loss.

4. Every loss is a multiple loss.
We always incur secondary losses whenever we lose a loved one. We lose more than our familiar routine: we lose our social contacts, identity, status, security, career dreams, sense of self, and dreams for the future.

5. Change = Loss = Grief.
Whenever we experience a change in life, we lose what we left behind and begin to connect with what comes next. Any change, even good ones, can bring about a sense of loss and trigger a grief reaction.

6. We grieve old loss while grieving a new loss.
As we move through the transitions of life and experience losses, we accumulate the loss material that was not processed properly. In spite of our previous grieving, some unfinished and unaccommodated grief may remain, and when a new loss occurs, the old stored grief mingles with the new and intensifies the grief reaction.

7. We grieve when a loss has occurred or is threatening to occur (anticipatory grief).
We don't need the actual death to begin to grieve; even the threat

of loss can invoke the grief response. Often the process begins well in advance of the actual loss event.

The Components of Grief: Psychological, Physical, Social, Spiritual

The Psychological Component (Jeffreys)

Sadness

The pain of grief is usually associated with crying, sobbing, sighing, blowing the nose, wringing hands, shaking the head, and verbal expressions of pain and hurt. Anything from soft sobbing to vigorous wailing can be expected.

Anger

A grieving person can be intimidating. The grieving person may scream, bang fists, slam doors or have hostile outbursts. Anger can be directed to anyone connected with the death, diagnosis, or other situation, God or a belief system.

Anger also has a quiet side. It may go underground and cause internal, emotional and physical damage.

Fear

Many grieving people will express specific fears and general anxiety as part of their grief reaction: I don't believe I can make it on my own. Maybe I or another loved one will die too. I'm afraid I will go crazy. Underlying all of these statements are fears about one's physical and emotional survival.

Guilt

Guilt is a normal and expected aspect of the grief experience. Guilt usually comes from the nature of the death and its possible preventability, or from unresolved relationship issues. Sometimes there is a clear and valid reason for the guilt, and in other cases it comes from what people believe they should have done or not done in the relationship while the deceased was still alive. Other times, the guilt has no rational or tangible source. However, grieving people who experience continuous distress and dysfunction due to complications as a result of guilt should seek the help of a professional.

Sibling guilt

Surviving siblings often are overwhelmed by guilt if they were jealous or angry with a sister or brother who was ill and later died. Siblings and parents alike may also suffer from 'survivor guilt', the guilt of having survived while others died.

Shame (often present in disenfranchised grief)

Shame is related to guilt, and people who feel shame are often concerned about their social status. "What would people think if they knew that my son killed himself?", etc.

Certain types of losses are more prone to producing shame: suicide, drugs overdose, criminal behavior, layoff, bankruptcy, divorce, AIDS.

Summary of emotional aspects

The degree to which grieving people feel comfortable expressing the emotions of grief is related to the emotional climate of the family of origin and their culture. Typically, people who were not permitted to express their emotions as children will have more trouble expressing themselves as adults, thus making the grieving process more difficult.

Cognitive Disturbances of Grief

Grieving people's thought processes are also affected. This occurs when an individual's inner picture of the old pre-loss world does not match the painful new external post-loss reality, thus creating a discrepancy.

Common cognitive disturbances include:

- responding sluggishly to questions
- difficulty concentrating
- memory loss
- loss of interest in usual activities
- loss of pleasure
- general numbness
- confusion and disorientation
- a sense of futility and helplessness
- uncertainty about identity
- crazy thoughts
- mental fatigue

Confusion and inability to concentrate will dissipate over time, but questions associated with personal and social identity may persist and require continued support.

The Physical Components of Grief

Health factors
All parts of our physical being are affected by the trauma of loss, but bereaved children and older adults are at greater risk for developing a variety of adverse health consequences.

Common physical complaints of grieving people:

- lack of energy
- stomach aches
- chest pain and tightness
- shortness of breath
- dryness or lump in throat
- dizziness
- nausea

- frequent colds
- sleep and appetite disturbances
- body change
- sexual dysfunction

The Social Component of Grief

Family and other relationships
Grief changes the individual's face to the world. Social roles, family relationships and identity are all modified by significant loss. Some individuals shrink from social contact while others overextend themselves socially.

Society and attitudes toward grief
Most people react in special ways to a person who they know has suffered a loss. Some individuals avoid them, thus giving their grief a sense of abnormalcy. Others are overly solicitous and seek out mourners to offer them 'should advice', which is not of great help either. Too often, regrettably, some well-intentioned people say very hurtful and inappropriate things to grieving people.

The Spiritual Component of Grief: faith resources and life philosophy

Many people suffering loss will turn to their belief system for help with death-related rituals, prayer support, comfort and advice on placing the loss within a greater spiritual context.

It's a time for families and friends to be drawn together and reach back to their traditions in an effort to get some sense of comfort and understanding. Others, in anger and frustration, may reject any notion of God, because they see their tragedy as incompatible with such a concept.

Grievers with no particular faith system may find solace and answers in a non-theological, humanistic philosophy of life.

The Different Stages of Grief

There are numerous theories on the stages of grief, but my favorites are the ones put forward by the two most popular experts on the subject; Elizabeth Kubler-Ross and Therese Rondo.

Elizabeth Kubler-Ross

After working with over 200 dying patients and observing their behavior at the last stages of their lives, the author learned to identify five major different stages of grief. To date, these stages remain the most familiar and referred to by professionals and the lay public.

Stage 1 – Shock and Denial
"No, it's not possible." "We need new tests." "The doctor must have made a mistake." These are all expressions of shock and denial and are common after experiencing a loss.

Stage 2 – Anger
There are two ways a grieving person may express anger: actively and passively. While rage, resentment, bitterness, irritability and violence are expressions of active anger, stubborn refusal to eat, and refusal to comply with medical treatment are on the other hand expressions of passive anger.

Stage 3 – Bargaining
"Maybe if I start being nice with people, this situation will go away." "God, I promise to go back to church if you heal her", etc. These are examples of bargaining and represent desperate attempts to change the fate of the person who is faced with his/her own approaching death or the death of a loved one (in the case of anticipatory grief, for instance).

Stage 4 – Depression

Isolation and withdrawal from family and friends often represent a final act to prepare for dying. Also, people experiencing anticipatory grief will become depressed after experiencing the roller-coaster ride of remissions and relapses as they enter into a phase called 'learned helplessness'. At this stage, there is a perceived absence of control over the outcome of the situation. The person comes to the conclusion that each attempt at recovery leads to failure, which in turn leads to depression.

Stage 5 – Acceptance

This stage is more complex than we think. People at this stage, even though they intellectually accept their coming death, may still remain depressed, angry, bitter and fearful.

To the latter, I add two more stages:

Stage 6 – Guilt

Few survivors escape some feelings of guilt and regret: "I should have done more" are words that haunt many people. Were angry words exchanged with the deceased prior to death? Most people are very creative in finding reasons for guilt. So many things could have been done differently: "If only I had known." "If only I had been there, this would not have happened."

Stage 7 – Sadness

Sadness is the most inevitable emotion of grief. It is normal to feel abandoned, alone and afraid. After the shock and denial have passed and the anger has been exhausted, sadness and even hopelessness may set in. Crying episodes may seem endless.

Therese Rondo

While Elizabeth Kubler-Ross talks about stages of grief, Rondo divides the response to grief into three phases.

1. Avoidance
   - a time of denial, disorganization, and confusion when a person is forced to recognize, acknowledge and understand the loss

2. Confrontation
   - a time of intense grief when a person is forced into experiencing the pain and feelings of loss as a reaction to the separation
   - reviewing and grieving; recollecting and re-experiencing the deceased in the relationship
   - reconnecting with old memories of the deceased
   - relinquishing or surrendering the old attachments, both to the deceased and the pre-loss world as they knew it

3. Accommodation
   - a time of diminished grief and re-entry into the world as a changed individual
   - readjusting and adapting to the new world without forgetting the attachments of the old life
   - creating a new relationship with the deceased; a new identity and new ways to function in the new life
   - redirecting and reinvesting energy formerly absorbed by the old attachments into new relationships, activities or causes

Certain authors and I do not concur with the use of the terms 'healing' or 'recovery' from grief, as it is not a disease or a condition that requires treatment. Some talk about a process, although this is not entirely accurate either. I would rather use the terms 'life phase' or 'stage' that a person has to go through and rise from, in order to enter into the new world without the lost loved one.

Stages of grief do not occur in a specific sequence as described earlier, and there is no timeline for their expression. Some people may jump a stage or two and in rare cases may not express any of them, which could have a difficult rebound effect later on in life.

Summary: The Basic Concepts of Grief (Jeffreys)

Attachment is normal

Attachment occurs from infancy throughout adulthood. Its purpose is to protect and help the individual to survive. Attachment affects the nature of relationships as well as issues related to mourning.

Grief reactions are normal

Grief reactions occur every time an attachment bond is broken. People occasionally need help to normalize their grief if under certain conditions it remains unresolved.

Reaction to Grief

Grief manifests itself in four ways: psychological, physical, social and spiritual.

The expression of emotional pain

Anger, fear, sadness, guilt and shame manifest as grieving people confront the reality of their loss.

The reconstruction of a grieving person's life story

Creating a new personal and social identity is crucial in order to function successfully in the new post-loss world.

Relearning the world

The grieving person learns to transform their inner representation of the lost loved one. This enables him/her to maintain a bond with the deceased that is consistent with the new reality, i.e.

maintain a special connection with the deceased that does not interfere with the making of other relationships in the new life.

Feeling debilitating guilt or anger

These two emotions are particularly difficult to overcome in the grieving process. Many bereaved find themselves plagued with the "would've," "should've," "could've" persistent thoughts.

Appendix II: Coping Mechanisms and Strategies

10 strategies for coping with grief

(Source: thelightbeyond.com)

Grief is a personal experience, unique to each mourner and unique to each loss. Grief comes in waves. Times of peace and calm are suddenly shattered by overpowering emotion. The following strategies provide a few suggestions to help you ride out the waves as you cope with your grief.

1. Take time out. In many ways, the experience of grief is similar to recovery from a serious illness; some days will be darker, and some will be brighter. Recognize your limits, and separate the things that must be done from those that can wait. Don't worry about keeping up with your usual schedule. If you have to cancel or reschedule commitments, people will understand.

2. Avoid making major decisions. Grief can cloud your judgment and make it difficult to see beyond the pain you're feeling at the moment. Impulsive decisions – to move or change jobs, for example – can have far-reaching implications for which you may be unprepared. If you must make an important decision, discuss your options with someone you trust, such as a friend or financial advisor.

3. Talk. Painful feelings held inside are like an infection festering in a wound – they need to come out in order for you to heal. When friends ask how they can help, ask them to just be with you and listen. Tell them how important it is for you to be able to express what you're thinking and feeling. If you think you need more than the support of your friends, consider talking with a professional counselor.

4. Express yourself creatively. Writing is another excellent way to express yourself. Try keeping a journal or writing letters, whether you send them or not. When words won't come, artistic outlets like painting or sculpting or playing a musical instrument can help you to communicate what's in your heart and soul. Creative expression can bring clarity to the turmoil you feel and insight into feelings you weren't aware of.

5. Honor your loved one's memory. Preserve your memories in ways that are comforting and meaningful. Enlarge and frame a favorite photo of your loved one, or compile a scrapbook of letters and mementoes from the good times you shared. Make a quilt from his/her clothing, or plant a tree or a bed of his/her favorite flowers to create a lasting tribute. Contributing time or money to your loved one's favorite cause or charity is also a noble way to honor his/her memory.

6. Take care of your physical health. Grief takes a physical toll as well as an emotional toll. Rest, exercise, and proper nutrition are essential to healing. Counteract a poor appetite by eating small amounts of healthy foods rather than large meals. If you have difficulty sleeping, try taking brief naps or just putting your feet up and relaxing whenever you can. And while you may not be motivated to exercise, just taking a brief walk now and then can lift your spirits and help you to sleep at night.

7. Avoid using chemicals to numb your feelings. A glass of wine can be good for the soul and help to settle jangled nerves, but overdoing it can bring a host of new problems. Attempting to numb your feelings with alcohol, illicit drugs, or prescription medications will only prolong the pain. Eventually, one way or the other, you must come to terms with your grief.

8. Have fun. Grieving is difficult, but it doesn't mean you have to feel bad all the time; in fact, it's important to take a break from focusing on your grief. Have fun when you can, whether it's reading a good book, watching a movie, playing cards, or resuming other activities you enjoyed before your loss. Don't feel guilty about it.

9. Plan ahead for special occasions. Anniversaries and holidays can be stressful times when you've lost someone you love, and especially so in the first year or two. Talk with family members about your concerns; this may be a good time to introduce new traditions to mark special occasions.

10. Reach out. In the beginning, grief may be so intense that you just want to withdraw or isolate. Soon, though, you'll be ready to ease back into social contact. Make a date with an old friend, or invite a neighbor to lunch. Or try volunteering with your church or favorite charity – you'll make new social contacts while you help others, and you'll feel good about yourself.

Other strategies that will help you cope:
Source: *Power Up Your Life & Make Stress Work 4 You* (Pierre Milot)

Understand what grief is and how it works
Normalize your grief: grief reactions are a normal part of the human behavioral repertoire and will occur whenever attachment bonds are broken or threatened.

Seek for spiritual support in your local community.

Join bereavement support groups.

Express your emotional pain: anger, fear, pain, sadness, guilt, shame.

Shop with friends; join a gym or a social club.

Practice breathing and relaxation techniques.

Breathing

1. The Rhythmic Breath

Without crossing your legs, sit down comfortably on a chair, hold your back straight and let your hands rest on your thighs.

Close your eyes and direct your thoughts onto the air that is coming in and out of your lungs while directing the breath towards the top of your nose in the olfactory zone.

Now, start breathing slowly while counting from one to three. Then, hold the air in your lungs while you count another time up to three.

Once this is done, breathe out slowly while counting up to three again, then extend your breath to force out the air left in your lungs. In order to accomplish this, contract your stomach muscles to crush the diaphragm, then start breathing again up to three, and start once more from the beginning.

At first, start with 3 to 5 minute sessions and increase the length gradually to reach 15 to 20 minute sessions at a time.

2. Kapalabhati

Specifically recommended to counter the negative effects of stress and burnout, this exercise deeply affects the nervous system. It brings about a hyper-oxygenation of the blood and a momentary CO_2 reduction, which has the effect of calming the respiratory centers. These centers, in return, relax the nervous system, thus creating an incomparable energizing effect.

Kapalabhati favors the oxygenation of the brain, stimulates endorphin production (the feel-good hormone) in the brain, restoring vital energy. Its effects constitute inestimable benefits for nervous, stressed or burned-out people.

This exercise is harmless because the arterial pressure always remains within normal physiological limits. Nevertheless, it is not recommended for people suffering from serious pulmonary or cardiac conditions.

Kapalabhati consists of forced, brief expulsion of air, each time followed by a passive air intake. Contrary to normal breathing where the inhalation is active and exhalation passive, the opposite occurs in this instance.

The exercise can be performed standing up; however, it is the kneeling position which is the most comfortable. The spine must be erect while the head is well balanced. The chest must remain as immobile as possible throughout the exercise. The abdominal girth, which comprises the muscles in the sub-navel area, is the motor of the exercise.

Thus, kneel down and sit on your heels (sitting in a chair is also acceptable, if you have a problem with your knees), with both hands resting on your thighs.

Straighten the spine, expand your torso, and concentrate on your abdomen. Now, release the abdominal girth until your belly hangs out and then contract it suddenly while exhaling abruptly through your nose (or through your open mouth if there is a problem with your nose). This contraction will cause a sharp expulsion of air from your lungs. Release the abdominal girth immediately, until your belly hangs out once again, while a certain quantity of air passively and silently enters through your nose and lungs.

The complete exercise consists of a succession of abrupt and brief expulsions of air, followed by passive inhalations.

In this exercise, it is the sub-navel girth area that is the most active. Remember that the most important factor is the vigor of the exhalation, not the quantity of the air inhaled.

The speed must be increased very progressively. At the beginning, the rhythm is increased in order to reach 60 expulsions per minute. When the exercise is well mastered, 10 expulsions per minute are added until a maximum of 120 expulsions per minute is reached. The expulsion must last at least 3 times longer than the inhalation. Three series of 120 expulsions per minute is a goal to be reached with a rest period in between.

Summary: Kapalabhati

Position
Kneel or sit on your heels (Japanese *zazen* position), with the spine straight and the chin down. The chest remains immobile throughout the exercise.

Exercise
- the sudden and vigorous contraction of the stomach muscles expels the air from the lungs.
- the controlled release of the abdominal muscles triggers the passive inhalation.
- the face and nostrils are relaxed during the inhalation.
- the air expulsion is three times longer than the inhalation.
- the amount and length of the sessions are progressively increased until three series of 120 expulsions per minute is reached.
- a one-minute rest is recommended before starting again.
- the minimal length of a session should be 3 minutes, but may be prolonged to 10 or even 15 minutes.

The most common mistakes are:
- to make the chest participate in the exercise
- to relax the spine
- to sacrifice the strength of the expulsion for the benefit of the speed
- to retract the stomach
- to be distracted during the exercise
- to raise the legs
- to feel light-headed after the exercise is due to the fact that you're putting too much emphasis on the inhalation, which is a mistake. Revise the technique, make the proper corrections and start again.

Kapalabhati may be a difficult exercise to master; perseverance is of the essence here.

Relaxation Techniques

1. Self-relaxation method
Comfortably sit or lie down, close your eyes and start paying attention to the sounds and noises around you without trying to identify them.

Repeat mentally the following suggestion: "From now on and all through this session, I will remain conscious of all the sounds and noises around me, and they will even help me to deepen my relaxation. Even the sudden noises will not make me jump, but will rather help me to relax further."

Start by focusing your attention on your feet while imagining that you can feel and see them with your mind's eyes.

After a minute or so, redirect your attention to your breathing, and imagine that with each exhalation, as the air comes out of your lungs, your feet become heavier and heavier.

Repeat the same exercise for ten exhalations.

Now, direct your attention to your calves and repeat the same process.

Proceed the same way for your thighs, buttocks, hands, arms, shoulders, etc.

Suggestions
Do not linger on a specific part of the body, but rather aim for a total body relaxation.

Choose a time of day when you can perform this exercise without interruptions or distractions.

The length of the exercise should be approximately 15 minutes or 30 minutes if you add the breathing exercise from the previous chapter.

2. The Jacobson method

According to Jacobson, relaxation is the absence of muscle contraction, which leads in turn, as a secondary effect, to the reduction of brain activity. This method is, therefore, fully oriented towards the reduction of muscle tension. It is particularly recommended for hyper-nervous individuals who can't keep still, type 'A' personalities, the over-achievers and those who suffer from RLS (Restless Leg Syndrome).

Often, for some people, this hyper-excitability phenomenon is caused by too much coffee, tea or chocolate which creates disturbances in the metabolism's absorption process of minerals such as calcium. When there is not enough calcium in the body, the nervous system becomes oversensitive and can cause RLS. Restless Leg Syndrome can also be caused by peripheral neuropathy, a kind of degeneration of the nervous system. In any event, Jacobson's method is effective against one's limb's restless sensations.

The alternate muscle contraction / sudden de-contraction has the positive effect of bringing a fresh and increased blood supply to the muscles and thus has a soothing effect on the overexcited muscles.

As for any relaxation technique, choose a quiet place where you will not be disturbed. The discreet playing of soft background music is, as always, recommended to accompany this method.

In a softly lit room, stretch out on the floor, or sit in a comfortable chair and close your eyes. Extend the right arm in front of you, contract it and hold the contraction until you feel a burning sensation or great fatigue. At that point, suddenly release the contraction in your arm, so that it falls down heavily on your lap. Once this is done, focus your attention on the growing feeling of heaviness in that arm. At that point, you can, if you wish, accentuate the relaxation by visualizing your arm buried under an enormous weight. Repeat the same process with the left arm, legs, thighs, buttocks, abdomen, chest, neck, etc. Try to accentuate or put an emphasis on the areas of your body where you usually feel the more tension.

In the second phase of the exercise, using the same process, relax even further the muscles that are already at rest while another part of your body is contracted; e.g., while you extend and contract the right arm, make a conscious effort to relax the rest of your body.

For maximum efficiency, the exercise should be done for 30 minutes every day.

Summary: Jacobson method

Stretch out in a comfortable chair and close your eyes.

- Extend the right arm in front of you, contract the muscles and hold the contraction until you feel a burning sensation or fatigue.
- Release the contraction and let your arm fall down heavily on your lap.
- Focus on the feeling of heaviness. Repeat the same process for the other parts of your body.
- For the last phase, repeat the same process, but make a conscious effort to increase the relaxation of the muscles that are already at rest while another specific area of your body is contracted.
- Increase the length of each session up to 30 minutes each day.

Appendix III: Abandonment and Separation Anxiety

(Source: Wikipedia)

Emotional Abandonment

Emotional abandonment is a subjective state in which people feel undesired, left behind, insecure or discarded. People experiencing emotional abandonment may feel at a loss, cut off from a crucial source of sustenance that has been withdrawn suddenly or gradually. In a classic abandonment situation, the severance of the emotional bond is unilateral. Feeling rejected has a biological impact and activates the physical pain centers in the brain and can leave an emotional imprint in the brain's warning system.

Separation Anxiety

Separation anxiety, a substrate of emotional abandonment, is recognized as a primary source of human distress and dysfunction. When we experience the threat of a disconnection to a primary attachment, it triggers a fear response referred to as 'separation stress.' When human beings lose a primary relationship, they may feel uncertain about the future or fear being unable to climb out of the abyss. This adds to the separation stress. When the loss is due to voluntary withdrawal, a common response is to feel unworthy of love. This causes people to blame the rejection on themselves. "Am I unworthy of love, destined to grow old and die all alone, bereft of human connection or caring?"

Abandonment Grief Process

Grief is defined as 'keen mental suffering: sharp sorrow and painful regrets.' What sets abandonment grief apart from other types of grief is the damage it does to self-esteem. Feeling left

behind, excluded, or deemed unworthy by a loved one precipi-
tates a collapse of self-confidence. As people struggle with the
personal implications of 'being left,' they may turn their rage
towards themselves. This can contribute to the intense depression
that accompanies rejection grief. The process of self-attack can
range from mild self-doubt to attempted suicide and leave a
lasting imprint on the individual's self-worth, causing them to
doubt their lovability, personality-efficacy and attachment
worthiness going forward.

In adulthood, being left or feeling abandoned arouses primal
fear along with other primitive sensations which contribute to
feelings of terror and outright panic. Infantile needs re-emerge
and can cause individuals to feel unable to survive without the
lost object. People may also experience the intense stress of
helplessness.

Another factor contributing to abandonment grief is the stress
of losing one's background object. A background object is
someone on whom individuals have come to rely, like a lifetime
spouse. As a couple, the spouses became external regulators for
one another. They were attuned on many levels: their pupils
dilated in synchrony, they echoed one another's speech patterns,
movements, and even cardiac and EEG rhythms. As a couple,
they functioned like a mutual bio-feedback system, stimulating
and modulating each other's biorhythms, responding to one
another's pheromones and addicted to the steady trickle of
endogenous opiates induced by the relationship. When the
relationship ends, the processes it helped to regulate go into
disarray and the life of the person experiencing the loss is
shattered and he or she may take years to recover.

Appendix IV: Defining Grief in Layman's Terms

What Is Grief?

Margaret Darte

(co-founder, Bereaved Families of Ontario)

Grief is a feeling of total disorientation.

Grief is lying on the floor sobbing, when it has never happened to you before.

Grief is waking up at 5:00 in the morning with that old newsreel of your loved one's death constantly running around in your head.

Grief is sitting in a group among friends and thinking: "I cannot tolerate this another minute, I have to get out."

Grief is going shopping and while looking at a peanut butter jar, bursting into tears.

Grief is the total inability to relate to the members of your family in the way that you would like to.

Grief is many powerful emotions, totally unknown to you and unexpected until the death of your loved one.

BUT

Grief can be a cleansing process of the non-essentials of one's life.

Grief can be an opening to something richer and better.

Grief is like a summer storm with horrible thunderclaps clearing the heavy air. If you allow yourself the right to grieve though, similarly, you may be able to begin moving forward. Unfortunately, society does not always allow us the opportunity to grieve properly and we will have to find a suitable environment that will let us express our grief without judgment.

I Believe

John Kennedy Saynor

(Genesis Bereavement Resource; www.genesis-resource.com)

I believe grief is a process that involves a lot of time, energy and determination. I won't 'get over it' in a hurry, so don't rush me.

I believe grief is intensely personal. This is my grief. Don't tell me how I should be doing it. Don't tell me what's right or what's wrong. I'm doing it my way, in my time.

I believe grief is affecting me in many ways. I am being affected spiritually, physically, emotionally, socially and mentally. If I'm not acting like my old self, it's because I'm not my old self and some days even I don't understand myself.

I believe I will be affected in some way by this loss for the rest of my life. As I get older, I will have new insights into what this death means to me. My loved one will continue to be part of my life and influence me until the day I die.

I believe I am being changed by this process. I see life differently. Some things that were once important to me, aren't anymore. Some things I used to pay little or no attention to are now important. I think a new me is emerging, so don't be surprised and please don't stand in my way.

Am I Losing My Mind?

Don S. Hunter

(Bereaved Families of Ontario)

When working with the bereaved, one of the most prevalent concerns in questioning feelings, emotions and reactions to grief, is the fact that we frequently hear phrases such as: "Am I crazy?" "Am I losing my mind?" Certainly the vast array of overwhelming emotions can be surprising for those in early grief. It can be frightening, intimidating and confusing. However, one of the primary reasons support groups are so effective in helping the bereaved work their way through grief is the confirmation of normalcy they lend when others share similar feelings and thoughts. There seems to be a healing which occurs when the newly bereaved discovers his or her 'unusual sensations, irrational behavior and thoughts' are not abnormal.

Here are some physical and emotional symptoms not uncommon for those in grief:

- a feeling of tightness in the throat or heaviness in the chest accompanied by rapid breathing. The person may feel as if she is having a panic attack and have no control over where or when this occurs
- an empty feeling in the stomach and loss or gain of appetite
- stomach pain and nausea
- restlessness and a desire for activity while experiencing difficulty concentrating. Focusing difficult and forget-fulness quite apparent
- being in a trance-like state, sitting and staring for hours
- feeling as though your loved one's death didn't actually happen
- dizziness or disorientation
- sensing your loved one's presence. For many, this is quite comforting
- frequent headaches
- impatient with the tedious day-to-day chores around the house

Feeling ambivalence toward surviving family can be surprising for many. However, we should keep in mind that grief is hard work and takes a lot of energy (as it does for other family members). You may not have enough energy reserves during early grief to tolerate caring for others every moment. Consider asking family members for assistance on daily obligations so that you can spend some time alone and take care of yourself during the first few months.

Difficulty sleeping or falling asleep and possibly having disturbing dreams or visions of your loved one.

Sleeping all day or feeling like you do not want to get out of bed and face the world.

Once again, just knowing that all these feelings and emotions are a normal part of the grief journey helps the healing process. No, you are not crazy at all. Perhaps, a little temporary insanity is justifiable here, however. Remember that you just lost your loved one and that it may seem unjust to you at this time. Acknowledging and working through these feelings won't necessarily make these trials dissipate magically in a few short days. Gradually though, healing will come.

About the Author

Dr Milot has published four books in French and numerous magazine articles on parapsychology and health-related matters. He also recently released a self-help book on stress management entitled: *Power Up Your Life & Make Stress Work 4 You*. The book is a condensed version of his popular stress  management program. Dr Milot has been teaching this program successfully for many years in private practice and through workshops and seminars.

Aside from being a frequent guest on live radio shows, he also hosted his own television series on parapsychology for many years in Montreal, Quebec, Canada.

Dr Milot is a therapeutic counselor who specializes in stress, grief and end-of-life management. He is also to date the only certified 'Guided Afterlife Connections' facilitator in Canada.

Dr Milot now shares his life with Christine. No dogs, no cats. They work on new projects and enjoy their time together between their three residences: Blue Sea Lake, Quebec; Martintown, Ontario; and Riverview, Florida.

Dr Milot is available for private one-on-one, telephone and/or online consultation. He also teaches, to both groups and individuals, a very unique workshop entitled 'Passing Through'. The sessions are meant to help understand, support and facilitate the grieving process involved after losing a loved one.

For information:
Tel: 613.703.9237
e-mail: pierremilotcoaching@gmail.com

AYNI
BOOKS

"Ayni" is a Quechua word meaning "reciprocity" – sharing, giving and receiving – whatever you give out comes back to you. To be in Ayni is to be in balance, harmony and right relationship with oneself and nature, of which we are all an intrinsic part. Complementary and Alternative approaches to health and well-being essentially follow a holistic model, within which one is given support and encouragement to move towards a state of balance, true health and wholeness, ultimately leading to the awareness of one's unique place in the Universal jigsaw of life – Ayni, in fact.